50 Ways to Create Great Relationships

How to Stop Taking and Start Giving

By

Steve Chandler

CAREER
PRESS

FRANKLIN LAKES, NJ

50 WAYS TO CREATE GREAT RELATIONSHIPS
Cover design by Cheryl Finbow
Printed in the U.S.A. by Book-mart Press

To order this title, please call toll-free 1-800-CAREER-1 (NJ and Canada: 201-848-0310) to order using VISA or MasterCard, or for further information on books from Career Press.

CAREER
PRESS

The Career Press, Inc., 3 Tice Road, PO Box 687,
Franklin Lakes, NJ 07417
www.careerpress.com

Library of Congress Cataloging-in-Publication Data

Chandler, Steve, 1944-
    50 ways to create great relationships : how to stop taking and start giving / by Steve Chandler.
        p.   cm.
    ISBN 1-56414-510-7 (cloth)
    1. Interpersonal relations. 2. Generosity.   I. Title: Fifty ways to create great relationships. II. Title.

HM1106 .C48 2000
302—dc21
                                                                00-057943

For Kathy

❧ Acknowledgments

I want to thank Steve Hardison for teaching me everything I know that led to everything I wrote in this book; Lyndon Duke for consultation on making a difference; Fred Knipe for all the many transformative suggestions; Kathryn Eimers for the elements of sense and style; Bob Croft for producing an audience; Nathaniel Branden for the psychology; Colin Wilson for the philosophy; Lindsay Brady for the gift of perception; Darlene Brady for the business sense; Jim Brannigan for the representation; Ron Fry for Career Press; Stacey A. Farkas for the expert editing; Leah Be for introducing me to Lyndon; Scott Richardson for the ongoing ideas and encouragement; Dennis Deaton for playing Martin to my Lewis on the road; Dale Dauten for the great columns and friendship; Michael Bassoff for the relation-shift; Terry Hill for the letters from France; Bill Eimers for making the introduction of the century; Stephanie Chandler for working the Net; John Shade for the best poem ever written; and Spider Hole for the music.

And last but not least, a tremendous acknowledgment to my dear Dr. Merlin F. Ludiker for the gift of humor. (Ludiker, like Quixote or Pickwick, ventures into fields he does not belong in. And his innocence and enthusiasm for "faking his way in" are characteristic of an inverse heroism that causes us to laugh for joy. His attempts to look good are absurd, and his attempts to cover his tracks elegantly reveal the foolishness of our own lives wasted by trying to live up to other people's expectations.)

We will now discuss in a little more detail the Struggle for Existence.

—Charles Darwin, *The Origin of Species*

❧ Contents

How to Handle a Woman

I remember as a boy going to New York City to see the Broadway musical *Camelot*, and I remember Richard Burton singing a song about the wisdom he, as King Arthur, had received from Merlin, his wizard.

The song, by Rodgers and Hammerstein, was called "How to Handle a Woman." As a teenage boy I had more than a passing interest in the subject, and I was spellbound by the quiet, dramatic ballad. I remember the song ending with the king singing that the way to handle a woman was to "love her. Simply love her. Merely love her." I was young but I remember that the formula sounded simple enough, and I don't know why I didn't just adopt it right then and there for *all* relationships in life, because it would have saved me a lot of unnecessary trouble.

It took me many years after seeing that play to get that formula back, but when I did, powerful things began to happen.

As I grew older and began to make my living teaching seminars, I realized that almost all of us forget to use this effective process. We end up having difficulty in even the simplest relationships because we do not use it.

So, how you handle a woman is also how to handle a teenage son and how to handle a customer and how to handle a business partner and, finally, how to handle any relationship.

But where we often seem to go wrong is in misunderstanding the mechanics of love itself. Because we associate love with feelings and because we associate the absence of love with feelings, we turn the whole idea of relationships into a "feelings" thing. Even (and especially) in the workplace. And that is our first mistake.

Because love is not a feeling. Love is a *creation*, and, therefore, love comes from the spirit. It comes from the highest part of every human being and it asks that we access our greatest powers of imagination. As writer Emmet Fox says, "Love is always creative and fear is always destructive."

Recently I received a letter from a man in Japan who had purchased audio tapes of a relationship seminar I'd given years ago. One particular image intrigued him:

"Boy, I loved it when you used the dead fish as an example. It's so true! All a dead fish can do is react. If you put a dead fish in the stream it just reacts to everything, every rock, every branch, every flow of water. Dead things react. Like you said: Live fish don't react, they create. They create a path through the water or stream depending on where they want to go. That's so great. Reacting is done by dead things. If we just react to other people all day we...are dead already. We're a dead thing responding to the life of the other person."

The solution to the problem is so easy and gentle: You can change everything when you make it your gentle practice to create rather than react.

The 50 ways to create relationships all come from my workshops and seminars on the same subject. These are easy thinking tools that have worked well for average people like me. Through the process of trial and error I have saved the 50 mental concepts that work the fastest and easiest and put them in this book.

Each of these thinking tools asks us to be creative just a little beyond the norm. Each one requires a certain awakening of the artist that lives in all of us. But to awaken that artist within is to learn how to feel joy again—in business and in life.

Useful though pessimism is,

it can't cover it all.

—Tibor Fischer, *The Thought Gang*

#1   Use the Element of Surprise

Experiments never fail.

—Dale Dauten, *The Max Strategy*

The element of surprise is a notorious military strategic advantage, and it's an even greater advantage in relationships.

Think back throughout your life. What are the best gifts you have ever gotten? What do they have in common?

Some people guess that it's the gift of time, or the gift of something handmade, or the gift of compassion, the gift of listening, the gift of service; the guessing goes on. But many people rarely see it—the best kind of gift anyone ever gets is the *unexpected* gift, the one they never dreamed they'd get.

There's nothing better in life than a pleasant surprise. I remember G. K. Chesterton's characterization of a spiritual experience as the one in which you get a feeling of "absurd good news."

When cancer research fund-raiser Mike Bassoff began to realize this, he instituted a program with his staff called "Innovative Thank You's." He realized that an expected thank you was practically worthless to his cause, because it is instantly forgotten. But a thank you that was *unexpected* would be remembered forever. So his team constantly experimented with thanking people in ways they didn't expect.

Mrs. Harvey Johnson lived in Omaha, Neb., and had lost her son a number of years prior to lymphoma. She was terribly depressed at the time as only someone who has lost a child can understand. Years later, she told the story of her son's death to Michael Bassoff, and he listened. Soon after the conversation, she donated $50,000, which was used to buy new laboratory equipment for doctors experimenting in lymphoma research. A year later, those same doctors had achieved a breakthrough in experiments they were doing on the blood of lymphoma patients.

Whereas most fundraisers would have given Mrs. Johnson a pen and pencil set or a wall plaque to thank her for her donation, Bassoff arranged for her name to get prominent mention in an article in the obscure hematology journal, *Blood*. The journal recounted the experimental breakthroughs made by the doctors.

When the magazine came out, Bassoff traveled to Omaha unannounced to present Mrs. Johnson with copies.

"I'm going to be honest with you Mrs. Johnson," Bassoff said, as the surprised woman invited him into her living room, "This isn't going to make you famous because no one reads this journal but hematologists. But there are, quite frankly, eight people who are walking around today who wouldn't be alive if it weren't for you."

Bassoff handed the stunned woman the journal and pointed to her name, saying, "You've done something very important as a way of honoring the memory of your son."

Traveling to the unknown

Access to creativity in relationships is right there in the unexpected. All you have to ask is: "What does this person expect right now?", and then go one or two steps further into the unexpected.

I'll never forget the one Saturday morning my college room-mate was rustling around and I woke up to see him putting on a tuxedo.

"Are you going somewhere special?" I asked him while rising up on one elbow in my bunk bed.

"Not really. Just over to Heather's apartment."

"Well, would I be out of line to ask you why that would require a tuxedo?"

"It's her birthday today."

"Okay. Fine. Are you taking her someplace really special?"

"No. I don't even have a date with her. We've sort of been having problems. We have kind of been split up for a while. I just wanted to take her a rose and a card and wish her a happy birth-day."

"So you're wearing a tuxedo for that?"

"Right."

"Why are you doing that?"

"I want her to know that she's still means a lot to me, and I honor the day she was born. That's what I'm going to tell her, and then I'll give her the rose and the card and leave. Because we're not really together right now."

I went back to sleep thinking he was insane and I didn't give it another thought until a couple months later when I asked him how he and Heather were doing and he told me they were engaged to be married.

#2 Turn Your Light On

This little light of mine,
I'm gonna let it shine.

—American folk song

I have a friend who, compared to me, has always seemed to have it together.

He's always been extremely well-organized with his time. A number of years ago when my own life was chaotic and out of control, I went to visit him to ask his advice on how to get myself as organized as he was.

We sat down in this living room, which doubled as an office. He showed me his daily planner in which he had a simple list of tasks on this day's page. He showed me how he worked on one item at a time, according to its priority, until the list was finished. As I glanced over his list, I noticed something strange. At the bottom of his list, there was something written in a foreign language. It looked like Arabic or something. I asked him what it was.

"Oh, that's code—that's code for my wife's name."

"Why do you have that there?" I asked him.

"Because if she happens upon my notebook sometime during the day, I don't want her to see her name under the heading of 'Tasks.' That's why I put it in code."

I told him I understood, then I asked him why he had put her name there this day.

"Oh, it's there every day."

"Every day?"

"Every day."

"Well, what's that about?"

"Every day I do something for her. Some days I don't have much time, so I do something that might just take a minute or two—maybe I leave her a nice voice mail message at her office saying that I look forward to seeing her that night. Other days, when I have more time, I do more for her—a nice surprise."

"Every day?"

"Every day."

I told him I thought I got the picture, but I still didn't understand why he did this every day.

"Because," he said, "in my previous marriage—the one that didn't work out—I left everything to chance. I left everything to how I was feeling. I always thought relationships were about feelings, so I waited until I *felt* like doing something nice for my wife. I waited until I *felt* like telling her I appreciated her. The only problem was that when I *felt* like it, she often wasn't there, and when she was there, I often didn't feel like it. I let myself live in total bondage to my feelings, and the relationship got worse and worse."

"What's different now?" I asked.

"Just me," he said. "In this relationship I decided to do things differently. I decided not to leave this one to chance. I decided that this relationship was very important to me, so I was going to make sure I treated it like it was."

I asked him if it wasn't a little fanatical to do it this way, where he would do something *every day* and have it be on his task list.

"I think it's worth it," he said. "There's never any doubt in her mind about how I feel about her. That's worth it to me. That's worth the two minutes I put into it. If you have 24 hours to live in a day, and you have a relationship that's the most important thing in the world to you, don't you think a couple of minutes put into it is rational?"

I had to admit he had a good point. And his key word was "rational." He created a great relationship with his wife because he made it his rational and conscious intention to do so. He kept his level of consciousness up. He turned the light on.

We can consciously create the relationships in life that we want, or we can unconsciously follow our feelings. Our popular culture always promotes the unconscious way: Just follow your heart. Just trust your feelings. But that kind of blind romanticism always seems to backfire.

In the end, how we *are* in a relationship is a choice. One choice (higher consciousness) leads to a happy life, and the other choice leads to the ongoing black magic of human mood swings.

How conscious of the choice are we willing to be?

How to bring the light

Relationships always get better when we raise our level of consciousness. Conversely, relationships always get worse when we lower our level of consciousness. I owe a great indebtedness for this fundamental principle to Nathaniel Branden, whose books on the human mind are, in my opinion, the best written contribution ever made to the art of consciously happy living.

Try to think back to when you first learned to drive a car. Most people can remember the exact car in which they learned how to drive—the way it looked and felt, even though it was many years ago. Why is that? It's the same reason why most of us, who are old enough, can remember *exactly* where we were (where we were sitting, how we found out, everything) when we heard that President John F. Kennedy was shot. Why is that?

Think, too, of when you learned that a family member had died. I remember hearing the news of my father's death from my brother. I remember where I was standing with the phone in my hand, in which room, the expressions on my children's faces when they saw mine, and it is a terrible, staggering memory frozen forever in my brain, every last detail of it as unbelievable today as it was then.

This kind of perfect memory occurs because our level of consciousness is so high when we experience these episodes that our entire mind is engaged.

The mind is like a mansion at night. When we want to, we can instantly turn on all the lights. There is no preoccupation and no distraction. There is just pure and complete light.

When we were first learning to drive a car, the same thing was happening—total, lit-up focus of the human mind. It's the kind of focus you can take to a relationship any time. Just *bring* it, like a pitcher brings his best pitch. It takes a little practice. But so does pitching.

Imagine, again, yourself first learning to drive. You're completely present to the experience—the feel of the wheel in your hands, the exciting and almost dangerous sense of the other cars rushing past. Now imagine what would have happened if someone sat next to you in the car and started chatting with you. What if he or she started gossiping about someone while you were trying to drive? You probably would have said, "Hey, please, not now, I'm driving."

Now, think of how you drive a car today. If you are like most people, you can drive using very small amounts of consciousness.

Only one room in the mansion is lit for driving. You can listen to the radio, talk to friends, yell at other drivers, even talk on the phone. There is no longer pure focus on the act of driving.

The same thing is true when we first learn how to type. We begin by sitting at the keyboard completely engrossed, learning to type. Weeks later, a friend can come up and talk to us and we can talk and type and laugh all at the same time.

This is the reason: When we human beings learn something, when we master something, like driving, or typing, or anything, we proceed to automate it. We make it unconscious and automatic. We turn it over to the robot inside so we can do the task while we're thinking of a hundred other things.

The problem is, we also do this with relationships. We lose focus. Once we develop a fairly safe and easy way to be with a person, we automate it. Soon it becomes how we are forever. We continue our relationships at a very low level of consciousness and then we wonder why they lose their appeal.

Relationships always get better when we raise our level of consciousness and turn on the light.

#3   Lose Your Self

Celebrity is a mask that eats into the face.

—John Updike

I don't know if I can think of anything more damaging to happy relationships than the very idea of personality.

More cowardice is forgiven in the name of "I've got to be me," or "That's just the way I am" than with any other misguided ideas. Much too early in life we decide that we have a certain personality, and then we climb inside it to die.

Great relationship builders are willing to continuously grow and change their personalities in order to make and keep new commitments.

People who struggle unsuccessfully with relationships are willing to abandon any commitment, break any promise, break any vow, in order to keep their personalities.

Personality is a damaging myth. It's just not true that you're stuck with who you are. You can be whomever you think you need to be. It all starts with your commitment.

I once had a friend who gave self-esteem workshops for a living. She lived in a small town in California. More and more often, big companies were bringing her to the big cities because she had a nice way of firing people up.

I'll never forget, though, the day she confided in me that she was terrified. Her worst fear was that someone in the audience would challenge her facts or theories and reveal her to be a fraud. She said she was curious about me for not having the same fear. She wondered why I wasn't afraid that someone who knew more than I did would reveal my lack of expertise.

"That's because I'm making it obvious that I'm already a fraud," I said. "I'm not trying to be an expert or an authority on anything other than my own life. If someone in the audience had better facts or theories I'd welcome them up to the stage to share them with everybody. I am not trying to be an expert on anything but my own personal experiences."

"I would be afraid to do that," she said. "I don't want them to think that that's all I have to offer."

"That's all *anybody* has to offer," I said. "And besides, what do you care what they think?"

"I make my *living* on what people think of me!" she practically shouted.

"Well, then, that's why you're miserable," I said. "That's why you're living in fear. You should try to do without that idea. Because the truth is you're making a living on the difference you make, not on what people think."

"I'm terrified," she said. "I'm terrified that unless I use facts and figures and studies, they won't want to listen to me."

I could see that her fear was running her life. It was even running her career. She was obsessed with her reputation, and that's always a deadly blind alley to wander into. I knew her feelings because I used to feel them myself before I turned myself into a non-authority figure.

The tomb of personality

I can spend my life trying to control my reputation—trying to control what other people think of me—but the problem is that when I try to control what other people think, I, myself, go *out* of control. Living my life this way is, in the novelist Richard Brautigan's words, "Like trying to shovel mercury with a pitchfork." Or like trying to nail Jell-O to the wall.

And so we face the inevitable paradox of good relationships: less is always more. The less I try to get you to like me, the more you like me. If I focus instead on my own small acts of difference-making, then my reputation will take care of itself. It won't be my anxious concern; it will be my pleasant surprise.

There is a bumper sticker that says: "Practice random acts of kindness." And it's such a good idea to do this! For our *own* good. And they don't have to be so random either. "Random" is used in the slogan because it gives it a poetic contrast to the more widely used media term: practicing random acts of violence.

You *can* plan out your acts of kindness. Acts of kindness don't *depend* on who you are, or who you've said your personality is. They actually *create* who you are. The acts come first and the personality comes second. Always. Yet most people live in reverse order, prisoners to their perceived selves.

Recently, I met with a musician who I was considering hiring to perform at a large event. In our talk over breakfast we found that we shared a love for much of the same music. As we talked further, I found that there was an old Harry Nilsson album he had not yet heard. I told him how great I thought the album was. On my way home, I bought a copy of the CD *A Little Touch of Schmilsson in the Night* for him and mailed it out with a note thanking him for his time at breakfast. I did not do this because there is something especially nice or good about me. I did it because I saw it as an opportunity to perform an act of kindness. And it took virtually no effort at all.

I've found that the more of these random acts I do, the better my life gets. These are things I never used to do. But as I studied relationship-building, I began to see the power of it. And I didn't have to wait until something changed in my personality to start doing things like this. I didn't have to wait until it was "in my nature" to do it. I just realized that doing it was "a way of being" that I was willing to experiment with, and so the point was to simply do it. Doing it is all that matters.

Through these experiments, I was able to lose my "self." I was able to realize that who I am is not who I am. Who I am is what I do.

#4 Think As a Creator

Imagination should be used not to escape from reality,
but to create it.

—Colin Wilson

In relationships, there are two kinds of people: creators and reactors. Creators create relationships. Reactors react to other people.

Creators know how to use the most complete and most human parts of the brain. And in doing so, they engage their imaginations. Reactors, on the other hand, use the lowest, most marginal animal section of the brain. They just react emotionally to other people.

Animals react all day. That's all their brains can do. If I look at my dog as he's lying by the fire, it never occurs to me to say, "He's thinking about the future. He's planning out his next week."

Because animals can't do that. They are simply stimulus-response beings. They just respond to what stimulates them at that moment. The smell of food. The sight of the owner coming up the walk. Their brains are like mirrors that just reflect the outer environment of stimuli.

They often do it in such a charming way that we assign them all kinds of human characteristics, but the one characteristic we cannot assign is the ability to create the future.

Once we start studying people who struggle with relationships we see that they are almost always trying to operate by using this low-energy, animal portion of their brains. They fall into the same stimulus-response habit that animals have no choice about. They have learned to get by on their least active brain section, and they just react and respond all day. Rather than creating the relationships they want, they react to other people.

It seems to work for them. It is a way of living that is rarely challenged. But deep down they know something's wrong. It's as if they were driving their cars around in a low gear and never shifting. They eventually get where they're going, but it never feels quite right.

Shifting is what makes everything smooth again. Shifting is what takes a person up into higher and higher gears of creativity in relationship-building.

To shift up, you just breathe in and expand your vision. Soon your whole brain is filled with the picture. It's a picture of the relationship you want.

Follow the sword master

I knew a woman named Mary Anne who worked in a seafood restaurant that specialized in bluefish and lobsters. Mary Anne was devoting most of her free-thinking time to wondering why her manager was such an idiot. When she came home at night she talked for hours with her husband about it. Her husband suggested many things, but Mary Anne didn't want to hear them. She was becoming addicted to being a victim. Addicted to reacting.

One day Mary Anne was browsing through a book of quotations that her sister had sent her and she came across a quote from an ancient Japanese sword master.

She said to me, "When I first saw the word *sword* I thought I'd like to take a sword to work with me and see if I could get my manager to take me more seriously."

But then she read that the sword master's recommended formula for winning the battles of life was to "enter into your enemy's heart and become one with your enemy so that your enemy is no longer your enemy."

"It's funny how that one little idea seemed to light me right up," she said many months later. "I just decided right there to enter my manager's heart, whatever that would take, and that entering her heart would be my new pet project at work. It was interesting what happened. I had coffee with her. I learned about her personal life. I helped her with some problems she was having with her son. I just made her heart my heart. I never had a problem with her again. My husband was shocked when I announced one night, after he had asked about her, that she was doing great and that I was enjoying working with her."

Mary Anne had, in one instant, become a creator. Creators are people in the habit of shifting upward whenever they start to feel down. Even before communicating with another person, they imagine the best relationship they can imagine. And then future conversations are all influenced by that image.

Reactors do the opposite. There is no vision at all until the other person appears, and then the reacting begins. The emotions kick in, and anxious moments follow: What if I don't get what I want? What if this person doesn't appreciate me?

The habit of reacting doesn't always feel like a habit. It often feels like a normal spontaneous response to reality. But it *is* a habit, and it's a habit that appears by default. Just like a neglected garden turns to weeds, a neglected mind turns to reacting. Reacting happens by itself when we're not generating a vision. If we don't choose to create, we cannot help but react.

Therefore, the first step in good relationship-building is knowing about that choice to shift. Being aware of the choice. I can shift up to my imagination at any time. Repetition of this awareness is like living with an on/off switch suspended in the air in front of me. The upside of the switch says "create" (the "on" option). The downside of the switch says "react" (the "off" option). That's why people who simply react to other people all the time can't help feeling turned off by life. That's also why people who create are always feeling turned on by life.

#5   Commit an Assault

Thinking is the hardest work we ever do,
which is why so few of us ever do it.

—Henry Ford

Sometimes the most obvious idea is the one that stays hidden the longest. It's a shame when that happens between two people who are having a hard time with each other, but it does.

One such simple idea is this: Thinking solves problems. Or as Voltaire said, "No problem can withstand the assault of sustained thinking."

This is especially true of relationship problems.

If the problem is one with your car or with your house, you quite naturally apply sustained thinking until the problem is solved. You do that out of habit, and because you know it works.

However, if you're like most people, when the problem is about a relationship, you don't do the same thing. You don't sustain your thinking, because the minute you begin, feelings seem to take over, and a voice inside says, "I don't want to think about it."

That's why counselors and consultants do such a great business in the area of people problems. They don't feel anything about those problems. All they do is listen carefully to their emotionally charged clients, and then apply sustained thinking. They have no emotional involvement with the problem, so they never hear the inner voice that tells them not to think about it. They are prepared to think about it until the cows come home. And that kind of sustained thinking will always solve a problem.

The people who actually *have* the problem are so emotionally wired up, they're no longer rational. A consultant can come in and help solve things quickly. Is it because the consultant is smarter than the client? No. The consultant has a different advantage. The consultant can painlessly think about it forever.

That's why it's so valuable to create an inner consultant's voice for yourself. An inner therapist. Someone you make up inside you who can give you the distance you need from your problem so that you can think about it. It helps to get this process going by asking yourself, "What if this were someone else's problem? What would I advise them to do?" Creating that distance allows thinking to occur.

A final method you'll enjoy using when you have a problem is to brainstorm with yourself. Take out a piece of paper and number it from one to 10 and then ask yourself: "What are 10 ways I could solve this problem?" Don't leave the room until you've written ten things down, no matter how weird some of them are. It will almost never fail to give you the problem-solving idea you need because it is an exercise that manipulates you into thinking. No problem can withstand the assault of sustained thinking.

#6 Release Your Butterflies

For of all sad words of tongues or pen the saddest are these: It might have been.

—John Greenleaf Whittier

In many of my public seminars, I'll begin the day by asking people to get up from their seats and go around the room and introduce themselves to as many people as they can in 90 seconds. We make a game out of it.

There's happy chaos that ensues, although the exercise usually begins with some tense, timid beginning moments. But once the momentum gets going, you can't sit people down. They're going all around the room laughing and shaking hands.

Most people, including me, hate exercises like this.

At least at the beginning. Because these kinds of exercises feel artificial and corny. Here we go with the woo-woo touchy-feely, I say to myself. I roll my eyes. I'm too cool for this kind of thing. But once I start to do it, I am having fun and feeling great. I have crossed some kind of invisible line. If I could only keep that invisible line in mind, that's where all great relationships happen. *On the other side of that line.*

The first day of my own kindergarten experience in New Jersey I remember playing a similar game called In-And-Out-The-Windows. We began as shy kids who didn't know each other. But soon the dancing and singing and locking arms with our partners to go under and through the "windows" made by other partners brought all of us together instantly. By the end of the game, all the kids had run together, locked arms, laughed, and danced. There was no problem building relationships there. We had relationships right away.

These two exercises illustrate a vital point in relationship-building. It's a point about risk. Without a willingness to risk, there can be no happiness in relationships.

Now I think back on the hand-shaking exercise. When I began introducing myself to people in the room, I felt self-conscious. What if I'm rejected? What if I'm bothering people? What if I *look* like a self-conscious person? What if someone doesn't take my hand?

But once the momentum gets going, it becomes fun, even joyful. People are happy to shake my hand and I realize that they had the same fears that I did. In very small ways, we were all taking a risk.

When I made my first audiobook a few years ago, I decided to take another kind of risk. Rather than give a hyped-up super-motivated reading of the book, I gave a deliberately laid-back, soft-voiced conversational read. The kind I used to hear when I was young listening to all-night jazz stations in Detroit. The DJs were soft and mellow. I wanted people to be able to listen to my tapes over and over without getting stressed out. I didn't want to sound like a former Ritalin baby, like so many of today's personal power motivators sound. I was also modeling myself after the best of the earlier Wayne Dyer tapes on which he spoke so softly and calmly. But I may have gone too far.

One reviewer titled his review of the audiobook, "Wake Me When It's Over." The *Library Journal* wrote: "Chandler's narration is soothing, which may inspire some and put others to sleep." Other reviewers also had similar problems with the tape: "This guy sounds like Garfield the Cat." "Do not drive a car or operate heavy machinery when you are listening to this tape."

"I guess the book is always better than the tape."

Yet the tape has sold extremely well. And when I asked the president of the audiobook company if I could *please* re-record it, he refused, citing the long-lasting sales history of the product.

He doesn't care how bad it sounds as long as it sells.

I know that there are a lot of people who will probably never buy another tape of mine again after having heard that one. That was the risk in reading it that way. But I also know of a lot of people who have thanked me for not shouting at them. That was the benefit.

Psychologist Dr. David Viscott wrote an entire book on the importance of risking. He established the very direct link between willingness to risk and human happiness. "If you cannot risk," he concluded, "You cannot grow. If you cannot grow, you cannot become your best. If you cannot become your best, you cannot be happy. If you cannot be happy, what else matters?" If we go through our lives without ever feeling butterflies in our stomachs, then we are suffering from a kind of death by comfort zone.

In our attempt to be safe and comfortable, we're isolating our-selves from the source of all happiness—personal growth. Every un-known person's hand I shake represents a small risk. But I need to consciously make sure I'm risking every day, or my relationships will die.

The great thing about risking is that we can begin with small risks. A compliment that I wasn't going to give you, I give. A thank you note I wasn't going to write, I write. A warm hug I wasn't going to give, I give. A new manager at work I wasn't going to talk to, I talk to. Every small risk expands my concept of who I am. As I grow in my own concept, I start taking larger risks. Soon the whole world is opening up to me and my requests. My com-fort zone is a thing of the past. My butterflies haven't left me when I risk, but they've become wings on which I can fly.

#7 Magnetize Yourself

People talking without speaking,
People listening without hearing.

—Paul Simon

Listening is the most powerful part of a relationship.

Listening is what we value the most in other people. Listening is what turns other people into friends for life.

Listening is much more powerful than talking. Talking is always overrated. (When was the last time you heard someone say, "Hey, let's ask Megan to come on this picnic with us. She talks all the time.")

Listening is what we value most in *all our relationships.*

The great writer Brenda Ueland once wrote (in *Strength to Your Sword Arm*) a short passage about listening that I've always read aloud in my workshops because it expresses it better than anything I've ever thought to say myself:

> I want to write about the great and powerful thing that listening is and how we forget it, and how we don't listen to our children or those we love, and least of all, which is so important, to those we do not love. But we should, because listening is a magnetic and strange thing.

A creative force. You can see that when you think of how the friends who really listen to us are the ones we move toward and we want to sit in their radius as though it did us good, like sunshine. This is the reason. When we are listened to, it creates us, makes us unfold and expand. Ideas actually begin to grow within us and come to life.

The next time you're with someone you care about, magnetize yourself. Allow all her words to be drawn into you. Take her thoughts down deep into the deepest parts of you that you're willing to open up. Become enchanted and spellbound by the music of the human voice speaking to you. Notice everything. Silently feel it, touch it, and see it. And watch what happens to your relationship with that person.

#8   Break Someone Up

If I had no sense of humor,
I should long ago have committed suicide.

—Mahatma Gandhi

When two people are laughing together, they don't need any systems for how to create a relationship. The relationship is already, in that brief moment, as good as a relationship can get.

When Victor Borge said, "The shortest distance between two people is a laugh," he was describing an instant relationship.

Humor is something we often forget about as we go through the workday communicating with other people. In fact, many of us have a belief that work has to be separate from fun. Work has to be grim and serious. So we white-knuckle it through our daily existence. We're hoping, I suppose, that maybe in the hereafter we will be able to lighten up a little. Fly around and share a laugh.

So we miss the opportunity that is always there to lighten up and fly around right now. To experience a little bit of heaven right here on earth.

As the great NFL quarterback Fran Tarkenton used to say, "Whatever you're doing, if it isn't fun, you're not doing it right."

This is especially true of creating relationships. If creating them isn't fun, they can always be created differently.

There is an elderly man that I see at the local post office almost every day. He looks to be in his 80s. And either he and I have similar schedules, or he hangs out at the post office all the time, because I almost always see him when I go there. The most remarkable thing about this man is that he *always* tells me a joke. As I'm walking to my car, he asks me if I've heard why "six is afraid of seven?" "No," I always say to his questions, so he can tell me the answer: "because seven ate nine."

At first I used to dread seeing him coming at me. I knew a new joke would be presented to me, and I would have to force my first smile of the day, whether I felt like it or not. But soon his jokes, all of which were so innocent and corny, began to have their affect on me, and now I can't even see him without starting to laugh. I actually look forward to seeing him when I go to the post office. One day recently as I was driving through town I saw him walking rapidly across an empty lot with a huge sack over his back. Is he homeless? I wondered. But as I saw how fast he was walking, with obvious purpose to get somewhere important, I began laughing in my car. All his jokes came back to me at once, and I couldn't stop laughing. It suddenly occurred to me that this absurd old man, this man who may have nothing at all, just might be the biggest difference-maker on the planet.

#9 Create a Friend

To make a friend, be one.

—Ralph Waldo Emerson

Sometimes my relationship seminar gets criticized.

People fill out evaluation forms at the end of the relationship seminar I give, and when negative evaluations come through, company managers show them to me with raised eyebrows.

"We wanted you to see this," they say.

I look at the evaluation sheet and the criticism says the person couldn't relate the course to business life.

"Excellent," I say.

"What do you mean *excellent?*" they ask. "We pay a fortune for this class and you think it's excellent that they can't even relate it to their work day?"

"Oh, they're just saying that," I say. "But you and I both know that how you relate to people is how you relate to people. There is no separation. The skills are exactly the same."

"They are?"

"They are. As someone once said: "How you do anything is how you do everything."

"Who said that?"

"A Zen writer..."

"That's what we're worried about!"

"...who Phil Jackson admires."

And then they're quiet again. The someone who once said that is Cheri Huber, a writer admired by many people, including Phil Jackson, a basketball coach who has had huge success by not separating basketball from life. Because Phil Jackson believes that how you do anything is how you do everything. Therefore, Phil Jackson coaches the whole life of the whole person, not just the basketball skills.

People who fail in business are people who try to keep their business lives entirely separate from their personal relationship skills. They are people who put everything into airtight categories and have compartmentalized their lives so much that they no longer know where to find themselves. Which box are they now sealed off in?

This death by artificial separation is absolutely unnecessary in the work place. For example, when working one-on-one with someone who is having a difficult relationship problem at work I can always help him or her solve it by removing the compartmentalization. I remove the artificial separation simply by asking, "If this were a friend of yours what would you do?"

Recently a company president was having some difficulty with his chairman of the board. He was anguishing over what to do about it.

"I don't know what to do anymore," he told me. "I don't know how to approach him on this. I want to take this company in one direction but he wants us to stay the course. I have no idea how to get my ideas through to him any more."

"Are you willing to try something?" I asked.

"What is it?"

"Are you willing to listen?" I asked. "Even if what I ask seems really simple?"

"Of course."

"Okay, then I want you to imagine the best and closest friend you ever had. Maybe someone you knew growing up. Your best pal. Can you picture him?"

"Okay. I've got someone in mind."

"Now imagine that you had these same business problems with that friend. Can you picture that?"

"Yes."

"Now tell me what you would do. By the way, what is your friend's name?"

"Tom."

"Okay, what would you do if this were Tom? How would you approach Tom with this problem?"

"Oh, that would be easy! I'd say, 'Tom, you and I need to block out a whole bunch of time because we're going to work something out. What are you doing tonight? How about an early dinner and leave open the whole night until sunrise if necessary. I'm getting us a suite at a resort. We'll do this in style, but by the time the sun comes up tomorrow, we'll have a new agreement with each other.'"

"How would you feel about doing that?"

"I'd look forward to it."

"Why?"

"Because there wouldn't be any pressure. It would just be me and Tom, just like old times, off together with no pressure. We could loosen up and not have to act business-like. We'd have the whole night to get to the point. We'd have fun."

"All right," I said. "So if that's what you would do if you had this problem with your best friend, then that's what I want you to do with your chairman of the board. Can you picture it? Can you do exactly that?"

After some resistance, he agreed.

"Just make him your best friend for a night. Because I promise you that it works. How you are with your best friend is *the best 'you' there is.* Don't be stingy with that 'you.' Give it out to people more often. Watch what happens. Look at the kind of agreements you'll get."

I saw him a week later and he was elated. He couldn't thank me enough. He said that my idea had worked "miracles."

"It wasn't my idea," I said. "It was your idea."

If we would use this *best friend* system whenever we are stumped in a relationship, huge doors would open up. That's what happens when we stop artificially isolating ourselves. When we're willing to take our best friendship skills to the workplace, miracles happen. How would I heal the rift if this were my best friend? What kind of communication would make my friend happy?

And that's why it's good to get as personal as possible in relationship seminars. People tend to learn ideas faster when they relate them to their personal lives.

The reason companies keep using the seminar even though I don't relate much of it to the job is because people get better on the job after the seminar *because* they have applied it to their personal lives. How we relate to people is how we relate to people. Look at a videotape of how someone treats his family members and you'll see how he treats customers. All of life is interconnected. How we relate is how we relate. Let things break down at work, and things will break down at home. The reverse is also true. Improve things at home, and all relationships improve accordingly.

#10 Give the Gift of Silence

*The single most important principle I have learned
in the field of interpersonal relations is:
seek first to understand, then to be understood.*

—Stephen R. Covey

There is a gift that I can give others that almost never occurs to me to give: the gift of silence.

This was taught to me by Steve Hardison. He is a personal coach who has coached professional athletes and business leaders, and, fortunately for my life, he has coached me.

Steve Hardison is as good a listener as I have ever been with. Half of his effectiveness in coaching comes from his ability to really tune in to what people are saying. When I am with him I sometimes feel my entire mind light up, like a big city at night.

Steve coaches his clients to respect silence. He recommends that you have certain meetings with important people when all you do is bring silence. Let *them* do the talking. Let them do the thinking. Let them really open up and say what they always wanted to say but were too intimidated by another's clever words to say.

Steve Hardison describes it this way: "When I am silent, the purity of self speaks to me, guides me, nudges me. When I am silent, I hear the purity of another's self. It also speaks to me, guides me, and nudges me. Through silence, I am learning things I never heard before. In essence, I am discovering that silence is a symphony of selves."

If I am on my way home from work and I know Margery, my teenage daughter, is going to be there, I don't have to have any special agenda in my mind. My intention can be silence. I can decide that I will not fix her, teach her, correct her, shame her, improve her, or advise her tonight. Tonight, I will be silent. She can talk and talk, and I will be happy in my silence. I will ask questions and I will give affirmations of what she says, but other than that, I will be silent. Silence is a gift we rarely remember to bring.

#11 Rise Above Yourself

When you told me you didn't need me anymore
well, you know I nearly broke down and died.

—John Lennon & Paul McCartney

Whenever I talk to someone who is having a tough time in a relationship on the job, I get a funny impression that I am listening to the words of country music.

You know those country song sentiments I'm talking about: "I've been hurt so many times, I'm never going to reach out again," or "I've had my heart broken over and over and over," "I don't trust women anymore," or "I just don't trust men." Songs with titles like, "Is It Cold In Here Or Is It You?" or, "My Wife Ran Away With My Best Friend And I Miss Him."

Country music in and of itself can be fun to listen to, and the really sad songs—the ones that express the poetry of lost love—are beautiful in their own way. But their basic philosophy does not offer us a very effective way to build the relationships we want.

We've already looked at the relationship trouble that comes to people who live their lives reacting emotionally to the behavior of other people. These people truly are miserable. They react all day long. They wake up in the morning and begin their day reacting to all the bad news on the radio or on the television, all the crime, all the injustice, all the evidence that they can't trust people. Then they react to other people in traffic, flipping people off, getting flipped off, honking as they weave their way to work. Then at the job, the reacting continues. A harsh word, an implied reprimand, a cold e-mail from management, and blood pressure goes up, breath becomes short, the throat constricts, and there is an unpleasant fluttering in the stomach. Soon the heart races and headaches form behind the eyes, all in the name of reacting. This is the toll taken by the daily habit of reacting. No wonder we end up resenting other people—no wonder we can't trust anyone. We hold them responsible for all these unpleasant bodily feelings.

What lifts us up when we're in the depths of reacting is a gentle shift; not a huge *change*, not a transformation, but a shift. Just like the gentle shift of gears in a finely tuned car. We shift up from reacting to creating. And one sure way to shift is to ask ourselves a simple question.

It's a question first asked by Ralph Waldo Emerson many years ago: "Why should my happiness depend on the thoughts in someone else's head?"

This question, no matter how we answer it in any given moment, gives us the mental perspective we need to start seeing the possibilities for shifting. As soon as we begin asking ourselves this question, we're on the right path, because we're leaving the low life of deep negative emotions behind. We're rising up. Far above the butterflies in our stomach, above the pain in our heart, above the tightness in the throat. We are up there now. In the mind. In the imagination. Higher still. We're in our spirit now. We're ascending our internal ladder up to the spirit. That's where great relationships get created. Way up there in the spirit.

During a break from a business team meeting, a man named Jason pulled me aside and asked if he could talk to me. We took two chairs at the back of the meeting room while all the others left to take a break.

"This shifting concept we've been working on really helped me in my personal life this week," he said with his sad eyes twinkling.

"In what way?" I asked him.

"Well, I don't know if this is too personal for you, but my wife and I had been having some problems. She wasn't exactly as romantic as she was in the earlier years of our marriage, if you get what I mean."

"I get what you mean."

"And so I was just an emotional mess about it. I took her lack of physical attention very hard. I was wounded, and I pouted. Can you believe that? I pouted like a 3-year-old boy. I wouldn't talk to her, I moped around, I took long walks by myself. I imagined that it was about me as a man, my attractiveness, my personal appeal. My ego was crushed."

"I have been there."

"And all of a sudden I thought about it while we were working on shifting and using the imagination to get this customer's business back."

"Good! Because what you get skillful at in business..." I started to say.

"....you get skillful at at home," he finished. "And how you do anything is how you do everything. So I decided to get out of my lowest emotions and breathe up into my highest mind, my highest level of imagination. I started to *think*, like a detective would. I went to the library and checked out some books on romantic love, but the key thing here is that I made sure they were all written by women. You know those kinds of books I mean about how to really love a woman?"

"I do know them, yes."

"And I started studying up on what these women were saying and I was shocked. I used to think that women were just like men in the area of romance, but they are not at all. When I got the woman's perspective I began to do so many little things, giving things and talking about things, amazing things I'd never done, and then, just like the books promised, the gears seemed to tumble, the door opened, and all of a sudden it was like we were dating again.

"I shifted. I shifted up into my mind, out of my deeper depression and pouting stuff down low inside me, and when I shifted, everything shifted. Just like we're talking about with customers."

What worked with that man's wife does work with customers and anyone else. Shifters who shift up from feeling to thinking are like painters. There is first an empty canvas, and then there is paint, and then there is a picture! And soon that picture is more colorful and detailed. Relationships are not accidents that happen. They are created.

#12 Stop Changing Other People

You can't change other people.
You must be the change you wish to see in other people.

—Gandhi

One day in a company long ago and far away, my boss came into my office and told me I should immediately clean my desk so that it looked more orderly and professional.

He said it was wrong for me to have a cluttered desk. I should look at *his* desk, which is the "right way" to keep a desk. Besides, he said, what if he has clients touring the building?

"Tell me when that's going to happen, and I'll clean it," I said

"I shouldn't have to tell you that clients are touring," he said. "You should keep it neat and clean anyway."

"But I like it this way. In fact, I can't create anything without a little chaos swirling around me. This desk is necessary to my creativity. If I have a cold and sterile, orderly desk, I'll freeze up. I'll lose my imagination. I'll become a neo-Nazi like you."

Soon I was mentally off and running about how a wild and disorderly office is a matter of principle to me, and how I need it to survive.

Before I'd made that defense, it might have been easy to clean my office. But now it was impossible. I made it a matter of pride.

This is true of all things we are made to feel wrong about. In fact, the worst way to alter people's behavior is to make them feel wrong about it. If you tell them they're wrong to be drinking so much, they'll get upset, slam the door, go out and drink even more. If you tell them something's wrong with them because they don't study enough, they'll go to the couch and study even less. If you tell them they're wrong not to listen to you, they'll stop listening altogether. It's human nature to convert wrong into right. What you say is wrong they will make right.

The other problem with trying to change other people is even more important. Let's say that somehow we *do* get them to change. The problem with that is, we're *still* not happy. We thought we would be happy if they changed, but we're not.

Why?

Let's say I've been trying to change some habit of yours for a long time. In fact, I've convinced myself that my own happiness depends upon it. So now you've come home and surprised me by saying you've quit this habit of yours, and you're a changed person. Am I happy now? Well, not exactly. Because now I'm as nervous as before because I don't know whether I can *trust* this change. In fact, all I can think about is, "How long is this change going to last?" I try to act happy for you, but I have that horrible feeling that this is probably too good to be true. I don't want to get my hopes up. I don't want to set myself up for an even greater disappointment, so I end up losing even more sleep at night and bracing myself by day.

Any time my happiness depends on something *you* do or don't do, I'm *lost* because I'm looking for happiness in the wrong place. Happiness does not come from you. It comes from me.

Happiness comes from my own actions and creative interactions. Happiness doesn't come from the actions of the other person in the relationship. When relationships are good, the happiness is brought *to* the relationship by people who are *already* happy. I can share my happiness with you, but I can't get my happiness from you. The most destructive relationship illusion of all time is that other people can make us happy. They can't.

However, our already existing happiness can increase by sharing it with another person. In fact, that's also how people change. By sharing a vision that is mutually inspiring. If you can get me enrolled in a vision of a temporarily clean desk that makes both of us happy because it serves both of our goals, then change can happen in an instant. Change comes from agreement, not from making someone wrong.

It's funny that in the many years I've been giving relationship-building workshops and seminars, the most common desire expressed by my clients is the desire to change other people. The very thing that makes relationships *worse*.

Perfect prescription for misery

You can begin a seminar with a room full of 100 people and ask them each to write down the names of people in two important relationships. One in business and one in personal life. Then ask them to list two things that would have to change to have those relationships get better. You'll find that at least 90 of the 100 people will write down things *other people* would have to do differently for the relationship to get better.

In addition to that, most of the questions I get during the *first part* of the workshops are about changing the behavior of other people. But most of the questions I get near the end are about changing our *own* behavior. A sure sign that the workshop has succeeded.

It is painfully obvious that most people think that for their relationships to get better, other people would have to improve. Other people are the problem. Sometimes I even fantasize about increasing the attendance at the workshops by calling the seminar

"How to Change Other People." (I noticed the other day that a new book had just been released about how to gain power over other people to "get them to do anything" you want them to do. I'm sure this book will sell quite well at first until the word of mouth catches up with it. The word of mouth will reveal that it is a perfect prescription for misery.)

Because in the anxiety to change others is exactly where relationships break down. Right in the paranoid and neurotic thought that we can change other people. It never works. In fact, it's even worse than that. It not only doesn't work, it increases the original problem. It makes other people *more* problematical when we try to change them. Because trying to change other people drives them deeper into their defense systems. It makes them get even more committed to the defense of their behavior. They get defensive when they feel criticized, and when they get defensive, they rationalize their behavior. Pretty soon, they're even more *proud* of their behavior. They've fallen in love with it. So it's now guaranteed that the behavior will have strengthened.

This cycle of defensiveness soon has two people feeling more and more separate from each other. The distance grows.

If you try to change people, they assume that you are saying that they're wrong and that what they are doing is wrong. It's a human habit to defend themselves against this charge and prove that they are not wrong—they are right. Therefore, in the process of defending themselves, they become even more invested in their own behavior. Before, it was just a tendency; now, it's a *principle* of theirs. By trying to change people, you've actually increased the behavior you don't want.

If it's change you want in your life, change what you *can* change—yourself.

#13 Learn to Do Picasso's Trick

All children are artists;
the trick is to remain an artist.

—Picasso

The reason all children are artists is because children instinctively use their imaginations to create with. It's a use of the imagination that unfortunately falls out of favor as the years roll along.

In a television interview on NBC that took place shortly before his death, the spiritual teacher Abraham Heschel was asked what message he would leave for young people. He replied, "I would say: Let them remember that there is a meaning beyond absurdity. Let them be sure that every little deed counts, that every word has power, and that we can—everyone—do our share to redeem the world in spite of all absurdities and all frustrations and all disappointments. And, above all, remember that the meaning of life is to build a life as if it were a work of art."

Not long ago, I was invited into an elementary school to give a short talk on goals. I noticed that the kids in the class were just finishing putting their art work away. (They were all doing watercolors.) So, impulsively, I asked the kids, "How many of you are good artists?"

And they *all* raised their hands!

"I am! I am! I am! I am! I am!" they said.

Then they started holding up their paintings saying, "See?!"

Now, I wonder if I had asked a group of grown-ups the same question, would I get the same answer?

I doubt it. In fact, I doubt if *anyone* in a class of adults would raise a hand in response to that question.

Can you picture the adults? Some of them would be looking down, some would be looking at each other, maybe one would point to someone else and say, "She is," with the other person looking shy, saying, "Would you stop it?"

We're good artists as children but we're not as adults. Why is that? What happens to us?

Something happens.

Something very definite happens to grown-ups that causes them to lose that creative belief about themselves. And the more you study human performance, the more clearly you see that children use their imaginations to create with, and grown-ups use their imaginations for something else entirely—grown-ups use their imaginations to *worry* with.

But what most grown-ups don't always see or understand is that worry is a misuse of the imagination. Especially when it comes to relationship-building.

Albert Einstein used to insist that imagination was more important than knowledge. He didn't say that knowledge wasn't important—he knew it was. But his point was that imagination is even more important. Because of how powerless a thinker becomes without it.

Most adults have forgotten how to use their imaginations to their advantage. In fact, they now use their imaginations to their *disadvantage*. They imagine a future that frightens them, and in the very imagining they hold themselves back from life and love.

Children simply don't do that.

Let me give you an example. Let's say I was talking to a group of 100 6-year-olds, and I excused myself, went out of the room to get something and came back with a little puppy in my arms.

Then I said, "Okay, this is going to be our class puppy. I'm going to ask one of you to name the puppy for all of us. Who would like to do that? Who wants to name the puppy?"

"I do! I do! I do! I do! I do! I do! I do!"

If I walked over to any one of the kids with the puppy and asked if that child would name it, I'd get an enthusiastic response. "Oh, I want to name it. Oh, Fido, no wait, Rocky, no Sandy." No child would have a problem naming the puppy, because children love using their imaginations to create with.

Remember when you were a kid? You made things up. You invented games and you came up with names for things and you created and innovated all day long. You were dipping into your imagination constantly and coming up with things that delighted you and your playmates. The situation never mattered. It wasn't the situation that inspired you. It was the immediate awareness of your imagination, living in your mind, eager to get used. You might have just been sitting in the grass with your friends with nothing to do, picking up ladybugs and looking them over.

"What should we call this bug?"

"Hey, you guys, what should we name this bug?"

"Let's call it koo-koo head!"

"No let's call it doo-doo head!"

"No let's call it moo-moo nose! Or poo-poo toes!"

There would be names and there would be ecstatic laughter. No one would be afraid of looking stupid. The more stupid, the better. No one would be afraid of losing face. There was no such game as *losing face*.

Now, back to the present, and back to the name-the-puppy idea. Picture what would happen if I brought that same puppy into a class of 100 adults. I might say, "Who wants to name this puppy? You'll be naming it for the whole group. It's our group mascot. Who wants to name it for us?"

No hands. People feeling uncomfortable. People looking nervous.

I might then walk up to one of the adults and say, "How about you? Your job is to name the puppy for the class. What should we call it?"

"Who me? Ah...well...shoot. What kind of a name do you want?...I mean, what are you looking for?...I'm kind of freezing up here right now. How much time do I get to think about this? I mean...do you want a silly name? Why don't you ask my partner here; he's the creative one."

This person is clearly worried. Why? Because most grown-ups automatically, out of habit, use their imaginations to *worry* with. Rather than imagining a fun name for the puppy, an adult imagines what other people will think of the name.

This obsessive worrying is usually the most common breakdown in relationship-building. Because relationships are created from the imagination. Good ones come from creativity, and bad ones come from worry.

A terrifying hormonal period

Just how does this disastrous worrying habit begin? Why don't we have it as children? What happens?

I believe what happens is something called high school.

Think about our time in high school. (Or, if you want, you can combine high school and junior high; for some people it starts earlier.) In high school, for the first time in our lives, we start caring more about what *other people* think of us than we do about our own thinking. For the first time in our lives, we switch the use of the imagination over—from creating to worry. We do this not realizing that (especially in relationships) worry is a misuse of the imagination.

Do you remember what high school was like? The cool guys in my high school were the least imaginative guys. They were the ones who had mastered the art of flying under the radar. They showed the least enthusiasm for anything and displayed the least imaginative responses to other people. They were cool. Really cool. When they walked through the halls, they didn't even disturb the air they were so laid back.

When I went to high school, we idolized people who had mastered "cool." People like James Dean and Marlon Brando—they were our idols. Brando was so cool, you couldn't even understand him when he spoke. How cool was that! How uncommitted to anything! We all wanted to be like that.

Looking back on those years we can understand a lot of what was happening. We were going through a terrifying hormonal and social period and we would do anything to get through it without too much embarrassment, which is to say without too much expression of the creative imagination.

Almost everyone goes through a version of this high school period. And going through it only becomes a problem if we stay stuck in those personalities we created back then. Those personalities were selected for survival, not creativity. Some people retain the habit of being cool as adults to continue to hide the fear of what other people might think.

I have read two books, each with the title *Is There Life After High School?*, and both of them basically concluded that the answer was no. Too many people never recover from backsliding from creating to reacting. Reacting to others simply locks in as a new habitual way of being.

But great relationships are *built* with imagination! Picasso pointed out to us that we as kids were born artists, creating all the time. We intuitively knew how to use our imaginations. How many of us converted it into a worrying device, and just left it in that mode?

If we remain unconscious to that conversion, we will remain in high school forever, using our imaginations to constantly picture worst-case scenarios in our relationships. Picasso said the trick was "to remain an artist." Anyone can do that, but they first have to convert the mind back to its original shape. It has to be consciously shaped as a creator of ideas, not an instrument of dread.

#14 Bring It With You When You Come

To love is to be happy with.

—Barry Neil Kaufman

The best way to build strong relationships is to bring your happiness with you. Have it on you when you arrive. Get caught holding it when you pass through customs.

The more common practice, however, is to arrive without it and then try to borrow it from every person you meet. Sometimes even to demand it. And then, when you don't get it, to complain.

One of the many problems that comes from having your happiness come from someone else is that you can't trust it to stay with you. Because you had no hand in creating it, you feel alienated from it.

I can't tell you how many times people have said to me (and probably to you as well), "If only my manager would start doing this, then I would be happy." "If only my husband would not do that." "If only my wife would..." "If only my company would start..." "If only my daughter would respect my..."

If my happiness depends on other people, I have *no* way of controlling my experience of happiness, because I have put myself in a powerless position. Let's say that I think I'm unhappy because my wife has a habit I don't like. "If she'll just quit that, I'll be happy."

I now enter the folly of changing other people: Even if she quits, I'm still not happy. In fact, I might even be less happy if she quits, because now the nervous part of me that made that habit "wrong" has just found something else to fasten on. What's wrong with others comes from the nerves inside of us, not from anything inside of them.

A woman wanted to talk to me during a seminar break. When she was sure no one else could hear our conversation she began talking in a voice just above a whisper.

"Well, my husband finally stopped drinking," she said.

"Great," I said. "I remember you said that was the one thing that was making you unhappy. Are you feeling pretty good about it?"

"Not really," she said.

"No?"

"Well, I don't really know how long this is going to keep up. I keep waiting for the other shoe to drop. I mean, I sleep less than I used to now because I'm so afraid this is temporary. And he goes to all those meetings. Who is he meeting there? This whole sobriety thing feels too good to be true. Someone is going to take this away from me. I'm up nights now like never before worrying about it."

You can see her problem—the other person has all the power.

When we have our happiness depend on what other people think and do, we have lost *our* chance for happiness in a relationship. Happiness will never come. Because happiness doesn't come from outside forces. It's a feeling we generate for ourselves inside. Relationships get great when we finally understand this.

Relationships get great when both people bring their own good feelings to the relationship and share them. That's why people who focus on personal growth are not self-centered. People who buy self-help books and go to self-help seminars are not self-obsessed, as unhappy cynics like to say they are. Actually, they become the true difference-makers of this world. Because they are working on the only thing they can possibly change for the better—themselves. They know that the better they feel about themselves, the more they can give to other people.

There's a great old blues song that I used to love that sums up happiness in relationships. The name of the song is "Bring It With You When You Come."

#15 Be a Dream Hunter

The heart is a lonely hunter
that hunts on a lonely hill.

—Fiona Macloud

Once I understand that my happiness doesn't depend on what other people do or think, I'm ready to learn the gentle art of persuasion.

Once I get it that I don't *need* to persuade anyone of anything to make myself happy, I can then learn to get good at persuasion. Things we know we *want* to do can be fun to practice. Things we think we *need* to do to be happy are a struggle.

No one understood the art of persuasion as well as Aldous Huxley did, and fortunately for us he was able to sum it up in a single thought:

"It is not very difficult to persuade people to do what they are already longing to do."

There's a lot to be learned from that one sentence. The ease with which we can persuade people to do what they are already longing to do is obvious. It's a secret that great salespeople already know. It's also a secret that people who are great at relationships know.

One time a woman in one of my communication workshops raised her hand and said, "I have a way of getting my husband to do anything I want him to."

The room grew still with anticipation.

"What do you do?" I asked her.

"Well, when I want him to do something, I just get him to think it's his idea." she said.

People laughed with approval, but in truth she was onto something, because what Huxley meant was exactly that. Everyone already longs to do things. Everyone already has a million hopes. Everyone already has dreams. When we learn what those dreams are, we can fit our own requests right inside them and both people can get what they want.

If I know what you are already longing to do, it's much easier for me to fit what I'm longing to do into that longing of yours. There is enough longing to go around. If we relax and open up, we can get in touch with each other's longing. We can then take this longing from our hearts and convert it into something we can both really have.

If I have no idea what you're longing to do, I have no idea what motivates you. And if I have no idea what your dreams are, I have almost no chance of persuading you of anything.

Great salespeople know this. That's why they care more about what they are going to *hear* in their first conversations, than what they are going to say. Conversely, salespeople who struggle are always concentrating on what they are going to *say*.

People obsessed with what they're going to say never end up really persuading, because they don't make an immediate good connection. They have to continuously re-boot. Their problem is that they're not hunting a dream; they're hunting for relief from their own anxiety.

The role of dreams in human life

The best professional relationship-builder I have ever worked with is fund-raiser Michael Bassoff. He's one of the most effective development directors in the medical world today, because he understands the role of dreams in human life.

When I worked most closely with him he was raising money for cancer research at the University of Arizona. Whenever a donor to the university was being discussed in a staff meeting Michael would simply ask up front: "What is their dream? What future do they want? What legacy do they want to leave?" Because once he knew that, he could set out to make the relationship with the university be a part of that dream. His system was as simple as the old barbershop quartet song that sang, "You tell me your dream, and I'll tell you mine." That song is a perfect formula for persuasion.

A salesperson only knows how to sell a product once she knows her sales prospect's dream. Once she knows what her prospect's dream is, she can fit her product into that picture, use the language of that picture, and end up asking the prospect to do something the prospect is already longing to do.

When my client Anne was selling the service of fully staffed on-site copying and printing to large companies and organizations, she would always wait until some kind of longing was expressed. She met with prospective customers and let them tell their dreams of not having to worry about copying, printing, and all the office hassles that go with it. "I wish I could just wave a magic wand and make all of that hassle go away," customers would say. "Then I could concentrate on the work I do best and not have all my time taken up by little breakdowns in the office." Once the customer's longing was expressed, Anne would fit the description of her services right into it, using the customer's exact words and phrases to describe what she was offering.

The heart is a lonely hunter because the heart will want you to do everything you do based on your feelings. And like most bouts of protracted emotions, those feelings usually end up as fear. In selling, it's fear that we will lose the sale. In romantic endeavors, it's fear we may lose the whole person. This is why the heart can end up lonely.

But the mind, on the other hand, is not a lonely hunter. The mind is a joyfully creative hunter. It is the instrument by which we understand the feelings of other people. The mind can hunt all day without tiring as it seeks to serve someone else's dreams.

The mind and spirit are where we generate true love. The more we use the mind, the less lonely we become. We learn the art of persuasion as easily as we learn to listen to music.

Truly ancient human beings will be able to recall that Pat Boone opened his song "Friendly Persuasion" by singing the words, "Thee I love."

He had the formula down.

#16 Cure Your Intention Deficit Disorder

That's not the electric light, my friend,
that is your vision growing dim.

—Leonard Cohen, "Dress Rehearsal Rag"

Finding your soul mate can be wonderful, but in the meantime, it is also as wonderful to derive happiness from *whatever* relationship you're working on.

And happiness in any relationship is yours to create if you begin by asking this simple but artistic question:

What is my intention?

Knowing what you want is often just as simple as knowing where you want to vacation. It won't always come to you in a dream. Sometimes it helps to just decide. Then you can plot getting there and plan on enjoying it. Planning a life of fulfilled intentions can be as basic as planning a vacation.

But during this vacation called life, our desires often get radically externalized. They get transferred to the behavior of other people. I begin to think that if I can control other people and get them to think and do what I want them to, then I'll be happy.

Why do I think this? Because it seems like all my unhappiness is coming from their behavior. But it's not, it's coming from mine.

I had a business partner once who was a very bright woman, but soon after our relationship began, she started talking to me about guns. Guns, she would say, are the biggest problem in society today. We need to eliminate guns. We need to sue the gun manufacturers and conduct a nationwide shakedown to eliminate guns.

Whether I agreed with her or not didn't matter. All she could talk about was guns. She wouldn't leave it alone. She was obsessed with guns, and she was driving me crazy.

Finally I realized that the problem wasn't with her, it was with me. It wasn't really *her* that I disliked; it was me. It was my own weak non-response to her tirades that bothered me most. It's always our own behavior that is the problem.

So I finally decided to get bold. I asked myself: What would I advise a family member to do in this situation? If someone I cared about came to me with the exact same problem, what would I say to them? I might just advise them to *talk to her* about the gun thing. And so I thought about that for a while.

The talk I finally had with her wasn't easy and it wasn't smooth. I was awkward and very embarrassed to have to bring it up. I stumbled around and told her how it was finally getting to me. I told her that I respected her passion on the subject, but I wanted to experience her passion on the subject of our business. I told her that I wanted that passionate side of her, which I admired, to be applied to how to benefit our customers. I also said it was a personal preference of mine that we not spend time discussing social issues on the job. Not that it was the *right* way to be, just *my personal preference.*

At first she was offended and argued that I was the reason society had this problem. I was refusing to face it and talk about it.

Finally, though, she saw that I wasn't trying to make her wrong about the gun thing, or even about bringing it up. I simply had different intentions for the relationship.

Soon we were having one of the best talks of our lives about priorities and devoting creative mental energy to the problems of our business. When it was over, I was very happy. I no longer disrespected my own response to her. I was now happy with my response. And the fact that she never brought the gun subject up again was really just a side benefit. The true benefit was finding out that my deep unhappiness was not caused by *her* behavior, but by my own lack of willingness to talk about it. Once I talked about it, she no longer bothered me at all. In fact, I liked her a lot.

Like all creative acts, the choice to create a relationship begins at the level of intention. What kind of relationship is it my intention to create with this person? What do I want? (With my gun-obsessed business partner, all I had wanted was a good, goal-oriented business relationship.) These questions always start us on the path to creating the vision that is so necessary to a good relationship.

But if there is no intention, there's just reaction. Emotional reaction to other people. It can be mild anger or mild disappointment, but it's still an emotional reaction. And it leads to a life of resentment and misery. Most people begin all their personal encounters with this lack of intention. And without intention to guide us, we are lost, as in any journey without a destination.

The good news is this intention deficit (that leads to perpetual reacting to other people) is only a habit, destructive as it may be, and it doesn't matter where the habit began or why. If we become aware of it, we can change it.

All that matters is our willingness to see the habit and accept it. Once we accept a habit, we can choose to leave it behind or not. ("You can't leave a place you've never been," says psychologist Nathaniel Branden.)

If you're a habitual reactor, the first step would be to spot it, be with it, stay there awhile, and see it for what it is. Not in a condemning or judgmental way, but in an interested way. In a fascinated way. Just like taking an interest in what your computer can do for you. It is equally beneficial to take an interest in what your *biocomputer* can do for you, for that's what the brain is anyway. That's what you're working with, a highly programmed biocomputer. What new program do you want to put in? A new program is nothing more than your conscious intention, and your choices for that are unlimited.

#17 Satisfy a Deep Craving

The most astonishing thing I learned about war is that men will die for ribbons.

—Napoleon

I like to ask people to try to guess what the deepest craving in human nature is.

There is an incomplete sentence in our seminar workbook that is a quote from William James, the great American psychologist and philosopher, that begins, "The deepest craving in human nature is the craving to be _____." People all take a minute to fill in the blank.

It becomes fun when people begin guessing all sorts of cravings, such as the craving to be rich, thin, happy, loved, immortal, and many others.

Once while teaching in Long Beach, Calif., a young man in the back of the room offered up, "The craving to be... disease free." The people who were sitting next to him moved over a little bit when he said that.

Despite the many guesses, sometimes we never arrive at what William James discovered.

The real answer, as discovered during a lifetime of research into human nature by William James, is the craving to be *appreciated*. Even James was surprised at how deep this craving went. Even he was surprised that it ran even deeper than the craving to be loved. But the more we look into it, the more we believe his finding.

If you speak to women, for example, who have divorced their husbands, you can ask them, "Why did you divorce your husband? Was it because he didn't love you?" "No", they will often say, "not really. He did love me in his own sick way, it was just that I didn't feel appreciated."

The most thorough and thoughtful studies of the effects of childhood experiences on our adult lives show that the feeling of not being appreciated causes deeper wounds than just about any other experience. Even psychologically abused children felt a certain sense of love. But they almost *never* felt appreciated.

When you express appreciation to someone, it's almost always a powerful experience, and one they'll never forget. If you say, "I love you" you can't be sure how it will be received. The context has to be appropriate for it to connect.

But everyone craves appreciation because everyone feels under-appreciated. Have you ever heard someone say, "I have a problem: Too many people appreciate me. It's stressing me out."?

Xerox this!

A few years ago, Mike and Bob Koether started a little office equipment company in the Phoenix, Ariz., market to challenge Xerox, and everyone thought it would be mission impossible. Xerox was huge and powerful, and the Koether brothers were not. All they had going for them at the beginning was a gift for hiring good people and a passion for customer appreciation (the very thing they thought Xerox had lost track of).

A few short years later, their formerly small company was dominating the marketplace and was way ahead of Xerox in sales.

A snapshot I always remember that explained their success to me was Thanksgiving time. As most companies backed off their work schedules and kind of wound down as employees got ready for the holidays, the Koether brothers would spring into a new kind of action. Without doing any "work" at all they had all the account people in the company put their feet up on their desks and call people to thank them at Thanksgiving time.

"We called every customer just to wish them a happy Thanksgiving holiday and to specifically thank them for their business," said Bob Koether. "We had fun with it, and we took our time. We really got into all the things we were grateful for, and all the things we appreciated about that customer. We explained how the customer was responsible for the success we were having and we thanked them over and over for choosing us and for the way they put in their time working with us. The response we got was so overwhelming that our people started looking forward to Thanksgivings just to kick back and thank people. I still have customers today remind me of the pleasant surprise they felt when the president of our company first called all their key people one at a time just to thank them."

To test this theory, you've only to try expressing appreciation to someone in your life you haven't appreciated in a while. Pick someone on the job or in your family whom you haven't expressed appreciation to in so long that you can't remember it. Watch what happens. Sometimes the results are so dramatic that it changes relationships forever.

Keep in mind that everywhere you go, all human beings you see have this craving. It runs deeper than any craving in human nature. So whenever you are wondering what to say to someone, think of something you appreciate about them and you'll connect at a deeper level than you ever thought possible.

#18   Relax With Money

Someday I want to be rich.
Some people get so rich they lose all respect for humanity.
That's how rich I want to be.

—Rita Rudner

Paying attention is like buying stock in something. If I pay attention to my desires, I am buying stock in them. If I pay attention to my miseries, I am buying stock in *them*. I'm always investing in what I'm paying attention to. The dynamic of attention is really that simple—you pay it.

My own attention for most of my life—no, for almost *all* of my life, was a spoiled, underdeveloped, immature, stimulus-response thing. It went wherever the stimulus was. Like a puppy, responding to whatever stimulus is out there. My attention was uncontrolled.

After awhile it became clear to me that I needed to choose a few priorities and stay with them. That was something I had never done before. So, I wondered, was I too old to change?

"We don't realize how short life really is," my friend and personal coach Steve Hardison said to me at that time. "If we knew how short it was, we would start choosing what's really important to us and then focus on that."

"But one of my problems," I said, "is that I'm not good with money. And that has led to other problems. I guess, because of my past history as a child, I don't think I deserve money, and that gets in the way of my behavior today."

"Not true," Steve said. "That's just something you have told yourself so often that it feels like a truth to you. But inner truth is a creation. You create the truth about yourself. So if you want to create a truth called *I deserve money, I enjoy money, and I'm good with money* then that can be your truth the minute you say it. Just keep saying it, and never say the other thing again. In fact, you might want to put a tattoo on your arm that says *HFM$.*"

"What would that mean?" I asked.

"That would mean *Having Fun Making Money.*"

It was then that I realized that age meant nothing compared to practice. Choosing what to practice, and then practicing that, meant everything.

But choosing where to pay your attention is sometimes tricky. Because many times what you want isn't really what you want—it's just what you imagine would *get you* what you want.

That's why a lot of people say "I want a million dollars," when it's not really what they want. The missing steps are the examination and validation of the intention. Is it really my deepest intention? If it's not, then it's not going to really drive me. Our deepest intentions drive us.

So it's important, if I tell myself that I want a million dollars, to ask myself this question: Why do I want it? Why do I want a million dollars?

To pay my debts and eliminate all stress concerning money.

Well, why do you want to eliminate your debts?

Because I hate having debts!

Why? What exactly do you hate about having debts?

I can't stand the feelings I get when people call me about the debts. In fact, what's even worse is when they don't necessarily call me, but I spend so much of my time worrying about whether they're going to call and what they're thinking about me and what they might do to me.

So what I really wanted was for those feelings to go away—those worried, anxious feelings I had about what other people will think and do. (That's why so many people first get involved in drugs and alcohol—it takes away those feelings—temporarily.)

But what if I didn't have to earn a million dollars to take those feelings away? I mean, if all I really want is to take those feelings away, why is it smart to do work I hate to do because I think that work would lead me to a million dollars?

What if there was *something else* I could do to take those feelings away?

Just take them all away

I remember once when I set up two old creditors on a simple and small payback plan—every two weeks they got something from me, no matter how small. It *amazed* me how happy they were with the arrangement. They even began contrasting me with people who didn't pay them at all and declaring me to be a person of great character and integrity. I was stunned.

Had I suddenly become a person of great character? No. I just discovered a shortcut to getting what I wanted. I wanted a *feeling* to go away. I wanted feeling uncomfortable to go away. So, instead of earning a million dollars, I created a tiny payback system that I knew I could manage. The words of business consultant Lyndon Duke kept coming back to me: "Focus on the differences you *can* make rather than the differences you would prefer to make but can't."

When I was able to relax about money, my relationships began to get better. That's why having money is helpful to creating good relationships.

And all "having money" means is having money. Having some money. Saved up. In reserve. So you can eliminate the fear and desperation that a person worried about money brings to a relationship.

We usually think "having money" means being overly rich. Having expensive showy things. But that's not what helps relationships the most. What really helps is simply having *enough*. Enough to feel safe and secure. So that money isn't an issue.

Dennis Deaton's wonderful book, *Money: An Owner's Manual,* unveils divorce statistics that show that more than 70 percent of the divorces in America are caused by money problems.

People think relationships shouldn't be about money, but they often are.

The person who only makes a little bit of money but always has enough to put away is in a better position to relate to another person than a person who makes a lot but is always in debt. A person in debt is scared all the time. People smell the fear on them. People then get scared being around them. Relationships suffer. When you have a solid system for saving and managing money you're more self-assured than a person who does not. Self-assured people can relax with other people.

#19 Think and Thank

There is nothing either good or bad,
but thinking makes it so.

—Shakespeare

When people decide to thank someone, to express appreciation, they usually don't really think about how to do it. They usually just do it, in some easy automatic way. But, with a little thinking, they could make the experience unforgettable.

Carved in stone above the entrance to many of the Cromwellian churches in England are the words, "Think and Thank."

It's a very good motto to live by for creating relationships. Because in relationships, most people don't think, and many people don't thank. So it's even more unusual (and therefore powerful) when the two are done together. Because when thinking and thanking are combined, wonderful results occur. (We've already looked at the power of appreciation, and now it's time to look at a way to take thanking to an even higher level of effectiveness.)

The first thing to think about is how specific the appreciation is going to be. The more specific I am, the more real it will feel to someone. If I say something vague and non-specific such as, "Oh, look at my darling little baby girl. What a saint you are. Daddy's little angel. Perfect in every way." The child is going to wonder who I am talking to.

If, however, I can identify something specific and say, "You know what, Margie, I really appreciated it when you fixed lunch for your brother and sister yesterday. That really helped me out, and they loved the food you made for them," then Margie can accept that she deserves the appreciation.

The best child psychologists make variations on the same recommendation: If you want to improve the self-esteem of your children, *catch them in the act of doing something right.*

One of the few things I have learned over the years as a father is that what is true for child psychology is usually true for all psychology. My children at home have been my greatest teachers in the art of building relationships.

The more we constantly practice appreciation of others, the better our relationships become. The actions and characteristics we appreciate tend to grow. The actions and characteristics we don't appreciate fall by the wayside. People we don't appreciate become people we appreciate.

So why don't we *always* tap into this deepest craving? Why don't we look all day long for things to thank people for?

The answer to that question lies in the lack of thinking that characterizes most long-term relationships.

Because when we're not thinking, we're subconsciously waiting for people to become *worthy* of our appreciation. We're waiting for the other person to go first—to change first—or do something first. By doing this, we diminish the happiness on the planet. We have a whole planet of people waiting for the other person to go first.

The "you go first" approach is not a thinking approach. It's a feelings approach. If you said things that hurt my feelings, my habit might be to go unconscious and react to you emotionally every time I see you. That might feel justified to me, but it's just not good thinking. It doesn't get me what I want. It gets me even more of what I don't want, because it prevents me from thanking you for what I *do* appreciate.

Good *thinking* will always lead to *thanking*. Good thinking realizes that appreciation is what grows the good in a relationship and starves out the bad.

#20 Shift Your Gears

*Do things for others and you'll find your self-consciousness
evaporating like morning dew.*

—Dale Carnegie

I once co-authored a guidebook with Michael Bassoff on fund-raising, and we called the book *RelationShift*.

Truly masterful fund-raisers, the ones who raise large amounts of money, always find a way to shift the relationship between the giver and the recipient. When the fundraising is done properly, the giver of the money is as grateful as the takes.

I used to believe this was only true of fundraising, but I've since found that it's true of all relationships. When you focus on what you are going to *give* to the relationship, things get better. When you focus on what you might *get*, things go bad.

In fundraising, I watched in fascination as Michael Bassoff would always seek to out-give the giver. If someone donated money to his cancer research projects, Bassoff kicked his creative mind into gear trying to figure out how to give back to the donor.

He gave them medical reports, meetings with doctors, tours of laboratories, help with their loved ones when they got cancer, visits to their homes, anything and everything he could think of that would be a contribution to their lives. I remember once when an elderly woman casually mentioned to him that she had never seen Disneyland. She had been a donor to cancer research. A few weeks later when I called Mike's office, they said he wasn't there. He was at Disneyland. He took her himself.

After raising unexpected millions for cancer research, he would bring a miner's scale to his public speeches so he could illustrate the importance of giving back. As he put little stones on one plate of the scale he would talk about donors giving to you. Then he would put stones on the other plate and say, "You must always give *more* back. You must always try to out-give the giver. Of course it never works. The more you try, the more they give! But that's how the whole universe works. You can't out-give the giver of universe either. The problem with most fund-raisers is that they're always focused on what they're going to get. Those people are takers. They end up raising very little money. If you focus on what you can give, you'll raise all the money you need."

Creating the relation shift

I later realized that great salespeople operate the same way. They make a shift all the time from being a taker to being a giver in whatever relationship they have going, even a two-minute relationship on the telephone.

The salesperson who struggles and doesn't sell much always ends up operating as a taker. He gets on the phone and becomes an ongoing apology. He is obsequious. He is sorry for having to *take* someone's time over the phone to see if he can somehow *take* more time in person to present his product. When he presents his product in person, he is soon apologizing for his ultimate objective which is to *take* the customer's money. All the way down the line, this salesperson is a taker. Of course he hates his job because who wants to take all day long? Who wants to spend the whole day apologizing for his existence?

A more successful salesperson is a *giver*, not a taker. She knows it, feels it, and expresses it from the first phone call. Because she thinks she has a lot to give, she considers the prospect lucky to be talking to her. She's about to set up a personal meeting in which she will explain further benefits of her product and service.

She knows that this meeting will be a gift to the prospect because she never wastes anyone's time. She offers interesting and useful information on how her customers can grow their business and prosper. She offers counseling on many questions about the business, and she offers a level of friendship, service, and commitment to the customer's business that other people just don't offer.

Because the successful salesperson knows this, she knows her presence is always a contribution. She enjoys creating contracts and agreements that offer fair prices and great service. In fact, it's her commitment to always go the extra mile. Her customers are always served far beyond what they pay, so even the billing process becomes a contribution in her mind. Is it any wonder that she enjoys her job and that people love meeting with her? Is it hard to understand why she sells so much more than her peers?

Most people have a hard time giving because they've never tried unconditional giving. They've done something they called giving, but it was really a form of trading. They would give and then put a lot of mental energy into worrying about what they were going to get back. The true giver never worries. Therefore, the true giver is full of self-respect. True givers can't be taken advantage of because they're not worrying about deriving happiness from the other person's reaction to the gift. Happiness is already present during the giving. Happiness is created by the giving.

#21 | Use Your Best Weapon

True love is a discipline.

—William Butler Yeats

Recently, I attended a softball game in which my niece was playing, and I was amazed at the behavior of the parents at the game.

I was really taken aback by how little the parents seemed to understand about human psychology.

From the opening pitch, to the final out, the parents I was sitting with began to yell at the umpires and loudly criticize their calls. Between innings, when the umpires were standing right next to the parents in the stands, the parents continued their criticism. The umpires began to lose their patience. When the game continued and a call went against our team, one of the parents melted down and began screaming at a particular umpire. The umpire told the parent that he was becoming a disturbance to the game, and impeding the umpires' ability to stay focused on the field. But the parent increased his shouting.

Finally, to the relief of most of the people at the game, the parent was ejected from the premises. You could hear a collective sigh of approval from the fans of both teams.

It wasn't long before another close call went against our team and another of our parents began haranguing the umpires. (Notice that the close call went *against* our team. Probably not an accident.) The umpire called another time-out and walked over to our section and politely asked that parent to leave the park.

I then saw our team's young coach pulling the umpire aside and apologizing to him. I noticed that some of our players, while running to their bench, did the same. The umpire was smiling and nodding. As the game went on, the calls were fair and our team began to get its share of the close ones.

As I left the school after the game, I had to wonder. Which behavior had the best likelihood of influencing the umpires to be fair to our team? Berating them or giving them encouragement? The umpires were just trying to do a job. It is a preposterous leap of paranoia to think a softball umpire is being deliberately crooked. The officiating job gets flat-out weird when parents attempt to control the officials' calls through verbal intimidation.

I spent some time in the Army in psychological warfare. One of the first things you observe if you study psychological warfare is that fear is not the most powerful psychological weapon we know of.

Most people are unaware of this and operate as if it were. Most people think fear and intimidation are the weapons that will control other people, but this is simply not true. The most powerful psychological weapon known to man is love. This is why, when you are captured by the enemy, you don't give more than your name, rank, and serial number. The more they know about you, the more compassion they can show, and there is no defense against love and compassion.

Notice that when you've done something wrong in a relation-ship, the other person often will not want to talk to you. They won't give you much more than their name, rank, and serial number. That's how people protect themselves during vulnerable times. The more you know and understand about them, the more you can love them, and they have no defense against that.

Fear is something people can learn to dig in against, but there is no defense against love. No one can keep it out, no one can fight it off.

(Imagine our softball fans yelling at the umpires, "We love you! You're doing a great job! We appreciate the work you do. You're wonderful!" Of course, it wouldn't feel like a real ball game. But the psychological effect on the umpire would be closer to what the fans really wanted because even crooked umpires have no defense against love.)

A recent devastating computer virus was transmitted by e-mail. It had the words "I Love You" as the message line, because the criminal hackers knew that of all the messages in the world, this would be the one that would be most likely to be opened, and opened first, before the person could get to any other messages warning them of the virus. "I Love You" was something they knew would be opened immediately by everyone—even the darkest pessimists and most self-pitying depressives would go right to that message. Nothing they could have written would have attracted people faster.

When the American psychological warfare units went to Haiti a few years ago, they dropped leaflets on the island to prepare for the landing of the regular troops. Did the leaflets try to intimidate the Haitians? Did they try to use fear? Did they say, "You better cooperate with the American troops or you'll be wasted"? No. They used the opposite approach. They spoke of compassion and understanding for what the people of the island had been through. They told the people that the Americans cared for them and were coming to help restore peace and order and civilization to the island. The Haitian people responded, and there was virtually no violence at all when the soldiers arrived. Love changes people's minds.

When we use fear on other people in relationships, we'll do all kinds of subtle things to try to control them. The relationships get progressively worse. When we deliberately bring love in, especially to those who don't seem to deserve it, the relationships always gets better.

#22 Be a Servant

When you cease to make a contribution
you begin to die.

—Eleanor Roosevelt

When the serving of others is done in a happy spirit, relationships blossom immediately.

However, when service is performed in the mood of self-sacrifice, the service is wasted. Anything we do out of a sense of obligation is not a gift at all. We're better off not even doing it.

Obligation does not build relationships, it wears them out.

How do *you* like it when you realize that someone who has done something for you only did it out of a sense of obligation?

If I've enjoyed a wonderful romantic evening with my wife and tell her so the next morning, how would I feel if she turned to me and said, "Oh, I did it because I felt obligated. It was my duty."

I would not feel so great. It was not the kind of remark I had hoped for.

Obligation does not create great relationships. Voluntary and creative service does.

Serve someone else's purpose. Find out what another person needs and provide it. Just for the fun of it.

Steve Hardison figures out ways to serve people everywhere he goes. Sometimes he'll see a little family struggling with their groceries in the supermarket and he will step up and pay for them. He'll stop his car and talk to a postal delivery person in a small neighborhood and ask which family is hurting right now ("People who deliver the mail always know," he says), and the next day he'll bring that family an envelope with some cash in it from an "anonymous" donor.

One day he decided to "adopt" a person at a nursing home. He realized that he and his children had no grandmother figure in their lives living nearby so he went to a local nursing home and found himself one. The old woman, who had no one in her life, was thrilled. Steve brought his family by and they simply adopted her. He was so happy to have added her to his life that he begged me to come by the nursing home one day to celebrate it.

"Bring your guitar," he said. "We're going to sing to all of them."

"I didn't think you sang," I protested.

"I don't, but I'll be there to support you while you sing. They'll love it and so will you. And I'll dance. I may not sing, but I'm a great dancer. No one dances like I do."

"Steve," I said. "They're in wheelchairs."

"Doesn't matter!" he said.

So one evening the two of us went to the nursing home and I went to the front of the room and sang and sang and sang while Steve danced with the old ladies in their wheelchairs. I'll never forget the sight of him hopping around and dancing and spinning their chairs around while I was singing. He had an insanely blissful look on his face and the people at the nursing home were obviously enjoying themselves completely. Up until then they may have thought they had seen it all.

That's what Steve is like. A giver. Whenever he has a spare moment, he gives. I've seen him leave anonymous envelopes of money in people's mail folders at the office. I've heard of him sitting with a depressed person for 24 straight hours just to listen and talk to them. It was sometimes a person he didn't even know before that.

But here's the clincher, for me. One time, years ago, I was telling Steve about my many car problems and he was listening, as usual, with great compassion. It was in the winter getting near holiday season and I didn't think anything else about it. Until one day one of my children called me at work and said, "Dad! When are you coming home?"

"Why?"

"Just...when...when?"

"In about an hour."

"Can't you come home now?"

"Why?"

"We're not supposed to tell you."

So I went home from work and as I drove up I saw in front of my house a bright new car with a huge red ribbon around it. I knew right away where it came from. Although Steve Hardison made a ridiculous effort to keep the gift anonymous, I knew where it came from.

Feel the power and the grace

Service of others has gotten a weird reputation these days. We seem to have lost the fun and spontaneity that can be associated with it. Somehow we now associate it with dreary servitude and shuffling around—a kind of subtle inferiority.

In truth, when service is provided with the right spirit, it's a pure joy. The endless energy and spirit that my friend Steve shows is proof enough to me. I never see him happier than when he's helping someone out.

President George Washington was known for signing all his letters, "Your most humble and obedient servant."

No one questioned his power. What they didn't know is where he got it: in his commitment to serve. He knew the power and the grace he could get from service.

Service is the opposite of inferiority to another person because in service, the other person can't touch you. You are so high above your emotional center, you can't be intimidated. When your focus is on service, you are in the most spirited part of your being and it gives you the feeling of having wings.

People used to ask Mother Teresa how she found the inner strength to live such a life of self-sacrifice. All of her selfless service to the poor seemed so unimaginable to the journalists who interviewed her. However, as she often said in her interviews, "If people knew how much joy I was experiencing, they wouldn't consider this to be a sacrifice."

People who serve are way beyond the opinions of others. They are not worried about what other people think of them. They are too busy serving. And, as my mother used to annoy me by saying, "Busy hands are happy hands."

Studies at Harvard University show that helping others has a measurable impact on the immune system of the body. Even *thinking* about reaching out to serve others has a dramatic effect. Harvard researchers had 132 students watch a film of Mother Teresa helping the sick and dying in Calcutta. After the viewing they tested the saliva of the students for the level of immunoglobulin A, a vital defense against the cold virus. They found that students who watched the film, no matter whether they admired the work of Mother Teresa or not, experienced dramatic increases in immunity. Then the students were asked to watch a film about Nazi Germany and Hitler, and the same test was made afterward. The immune systems were depressed after the Nazi movie. This experiment has been called "The Mother Teresa Effect" ever since, because it has helped scientists explain why people who are serving others live so much longer.

Dr. Allen Luks created a breakthrough study of what he called "helper's high"—the rush of endorphins into the brain that people get when they help other people. He compared it favorably to runner's high, and demonstrated that people who are in the act of helping others receive profound physiological and psychological benefits.

Meditation expert Dr. Herbert Benson also concluded that helping others gave the same kind of relief from stress that meditation gave, if not more.

Once when meeting with the Dalai Lama, Benson asked the famous holy man what one could do to maintain inner peace and joy once the meditating was over and it was time to go out into the chaotic world. The Dalai Lama replied simply, "Look at what's in front of you."

In the years that followed that conversation, Benson pondered that answer.

"For a while I wasn't sure what he meant," said Benson. "Then I realized that by looking at what's in front of you, you attach your thoughts to other persons. That breaks the message of stress. And now I see that a way to make that really happen for a lengthy period is through helping."

Serving others breaks the message of stress because stress comes from focusing on personal worries. The more I worry about myself, the more worried I become and soon I am even worried that I might be worrying too much.

But the moment I shift that focus to what's in front of me, I see someone who could use some help. And the more I help, the higher I get. That's the huge personal benefit to making a difference in another person's life.

#23 Astonish Someone

Attempt the impossible,
in order to improve your work.

—Bette Davis

Once you've mastered the art of the unexpected, you are ready to take it up another notch to—the art of astonishment.

There is no way to overestimate the power of the element of surprise. If it's good for the military, it will be even better for relationship-building.

Let's see how this applies to how we treat customers, keeping in mind that customer relations is just human relations in disguise.

Customer relations in America has fortunately taken a turn for the better. In the 1940s and 50s the operative slogan for customer relations was "The customer is always right."

But it's not too hard to see why that slogan didn't last very long. It's a statement that's simply not true. The customer is *not* always right. The customer is often a jerk—but you don't want to have *that* be your slogan, either, so we moved up to the more functional mission of *customer satisfaction*.

However, in the highly competitive global marketplace, the idea of customer satisfaction began to run down. Somehow there was something inadequate about it. Soon it became clear—satisfaction is simply not enough. Satisfied customers don't build our businesses because satisfied customers don't talk—they are silent.

Satisfied customers are flatliners. Why? Because people today *expect* to be satisfied. If they are satisfied, they are quiet. It's when they're *not* satisfied that they talk.

Today's customers will deliver the most precious advertising of all—word of mouth—only when we go *beyond* satisfaction. We must truly delight the customer if we want the customer to talk.

I had been giving seminars in customer delight for a long time when a homebuilder by the name of Gary Gietz took my course and decided it wasn't exciting enough for him. He absorbed everything taught, then he took it to a whole new dimension by insisting that his company, Gary Gietz Master Builders, shoot for *customer astonishment.* By holding his company to that standard—we will astonish each and every customer with what we do—he has rapidly become one of the premier luxury homebuilders in the southwestern United States.

But he has also attained something else that I consider even more valuable. He has put people in touch with their formerly hidden creativity. By teaching his people (and even his vendors) how to astonish other people, he created a game that people loved playing. He transformed the thinking of everyone who came in contact with him. Astonishment became a way to have fun. It became a way for everyone associated with Gary to awaken the artist within.

They always figured out what the customer expected, and then brainstormed it further. How can we astonish this person? Soon they were coming up with all kinds of ways. Projects were finished way ahead of time. Extra flourishes were put into the building. Flowers were left in strategic places during a tour of the finished home. All things, little or big, are always a pleasant surprise.

How to attempt the impossible

Gary Gietz had created a group of co-workers and vendors he called his Astonishment Leadership group, and they met constantly looking for ways to astonish customers and community members. One day they heard about a 29-year-old man named Scott Anderson who was dying of colon cancer.

While Scott had been staying at his mother's home trying to cope with the cancer, his own home had been badly trashed and damaged. The damaged house was the one he had grown up in and lived in for most of his life.

Scott Anderson's aunt contacted a local newspaper and told them she was able to raise money for some of the materials necessary to refurbish the house so that Scott could spend his final days there, where he wanted to die. But she had no way of getting it ready in time for him, and Scott's days were running out.

Gary Gietz saw the little story in the newspaper and leaped into action. He mobilized his Astonishment Leadership team and they rushed to the original home of Scott Anderson to begin work. Within days, the team had renovated the house and turned it into the wonderful home that Scott had remembered and loved.

Two weeks after being granted his final wish and returning to his boyhood home, Scott Anderson died. Scott's 3-year-old daughter Ashley was not told immediately of his death, and went off to her pre-school dressed like a princess for that night's trick-or-tricking. Later, when she was told, she drew a picture for her daddy and attached it to a balloon that family members helped her release into the sky.

In reporting his death, the local newspaper said that Anderson never would have gotten his wish to die in his boyhood home "if it hadn't been for a group of people calling themselves the Astonishment Leadership Service. Paint, hammers, and a lot of heart later, the house was renovated in time to grant Anderson his wish."

To honor Gary's group, Anderson's mother placed a plaque at the front door of his home that simply read, "Astonishment House."

"It will be Ashley's some day," Anderson's mother said.

I once sat in on one of Gary's Astonishment Leadership group meetings and at one point in the meeting, as a mental exercise, we went around the room and declared *who we were* at the core—what our basic commitment was. When it came to Gary's turn, he said that he was "love." To those who did not know his work, that would have seemed very corny. A lot of eyes would have rolled upward. But those who were there knew him and his track record, and when he said he was "love," people simply nodded as if they already knew that.

When studying Gary and his work, it's easy to see that the power of astonishment doesn't just apply to business. It applies to any relationship. If I look at how to astonish the people I relate to, I'm always looking at bringing out the best of me.

#24 Throw Out a Safety Net

Love is always creative,
and fear is always destructive.

—Emmet Fox

"What if I think I'm a very good listener," a woman asked me, "but I have someone in my life who doesn't want to talk. He just doesn't want to tell me how he's feeling or what he wants, or even what his dreams are."

I suggested to her that the way to understand people like that is to understand their fear. People spend their whole lives trying to hide their fear from us, but fear is almost always the cause of strange behavior. Especially with someone who won't open up.

The only way I know to create a conversation with someone who won't open up is to open *myself* up even more. I realize I need to make it feel safer for the other person to talk.

To make the conversation feel safer, I might want to keep looking for things I can reveal about my own fears and problems. No one can relate to a person who's got it all together. No one can relate to a person who is right about everything. And no one can relate to a person who pretends to know no fear. So I like to do my best to remember the very worst things I've ever felt and done and start talking about them. Sometimes people start laughing and say, "Well, I'm not *that* bad."

"If someone isn't talking to you," I said to the woman who had a problem, "maybe you haven't made it safe yet."

That's part of the real fun of creating relationships. Figuring out what you can do to open people up. Finding the right story in your own past that sets them free to talk.

When I first started working with Steve Hardison, I remember trying to get up the courage to tell him about some of the messes I had made of my life during my younger days when I was drinking and causing trouble everywhere I went.

He could see that it was hard for me to talk about these things, so he stopped me.

"Okay, I understand. Is it okay if I talk about something else for a minute?" he asked.

"Sure," I said, glad to be changing the subject.

And then Steve launched into a series of stories that stood my hair on end. Stories from his own life about ways he had strayed from the straight and narrow as a wild youth. I was stunned. Because here he was, a business consultant impeccably dressed and respected by top CEOs across the world, and he was describing a past that sounded like the script to *Rebel Without A Cause*. By the time he was finished, I was liberated! I was free to talk, and, boy, did I want to. Because here was a person who would understand.

"There isn't anything you could tell me about yourself that would cause me to think poorly of you," Steve laughed. "There isn't anything you've ever done or thought about doing that would ever reduce my commitment to you, my love for you, and my promise to help you become as great as you can be. Nothing would shock me. Nothing would be a negative to me. Ever."

And it was at that moment that I opened up and became more or less teachable.

#25 Climb Your Ladder

We have done with hope and honor,
We are lost to love and truth,
We are dropping down the ladder rung by rung.

—Rudyard Kipling

There's a ladder inside all of us.

It's called the ladder of selves. It's a ladder I talk about in most of my courses and write about in most of my books because it always applies to the subject at hand. And people almost always become interested in using it.

People use it as a mental picture. It takes exactly one second to use.

On the lower rungs of the ladder we have our lowest selves—the ones that require the lowest levels of consciousness. These low selves are our physical selves. We activate these personalities in us when, for example, when we're walking down a dark street at night and someone jumps out at us. We can physically run or we can physically fight. We can activate our "feets don't fail me now" self, or we can activate our Jackie Chan self. But whichever physical self we activate, it does not require a lot of creative or strategic thinking.

As we go up the ladder, past the physical self, we find our emotional selves. We blindly reach out and find the rungs on the ladder for fear, guilt, anger, resentment, and as we go a little higher up, we find the positive emotions: contentment, enjoyment, euphoria, and so on. These middle rungs on the ladder, the emotional selves, take more consciousness than the physical selves, but not much more. It is from these emotional selves that most relationships are maintained, which is why most relationships are so unsatisfactory.

We usually communicate to each other from emotional self to emotional self without even realizing it. My fear talks to your anger. Your anger talks back to my fear.

"What can I do to make you feel better?"

"Nothing; it's not about you. Why do you think you can control other people's feelings? That's part of the problem we're having here. You've got to know that you can't just talk your way out of things. Sometimes you have to do something."

"What do you want me to do?"

"That's just it! If you're doing it because I want you to, then you're still not taking any responsibility. You're just trying to placate my moods. You are effectively trying to make every problem we have be my problem. It's always made to look like it's me. It's not that anything's really wrong, it's just that I can't handle it. I would love it if just once you would realize *on your own* that something is really wrong and then do something about it. Instead, you wait and wait until I finally blow up emotionally, and then you have the problem be my emotions. As always, you get to be the saint. I'm tired of that! You can take a hike!"

Although we put words and phrases to these emotions, we aren't really communicating. Not in the highest sense. Not in the sense that we've created a solution or an agreement together. That's why relationship problems often go unresolved. There's no imaginative thinking going on—only feeling.

Going up to love and truth

As we travel higher on the ladder, we get to the best part. The highest level is the mind: thoughtfulness, mindfulness, imagination, and creative thinking. If we go even further up the ladder, we reach the very top rung which is pure spirit. Great relationships are created from the highest rungs on the ladder. Relationship problems always get solved by going up the ladder, and relationship problems always get worse by going down the ladder.

A perfect example of being way up on the highest rungs of the ladder is during courtship. If you've ever fallen in love and romanced someone, you know how to go up your ladder. In courtship, you were in your most clever, thoughtful, amusing, and strategic personalities. You were accessing your highest consciousness. Contrary to the common folk-wisdom in our society, you were not operating from the heart, you were operating from the mind.

Most people believe that they are sent up and down the ladder because of someone else's behavior. They talk about their relationships as if they were all on some terrifying elevator ride from the movie *Speed* with a demented Dennis Hopper ready to cut the cables at any given moment. Unfortunately, that's how most people experience life. But that experience is a choice. We can also choose to know about the ladder, and to learn to push our *own* elevator buttons.

People who love the thrill of courtship will sometimes misinterpret how they got that thrill. They'll think it was because of the new exciting experience and the new exciting person they fell in love with. But it's not that at all.

It's all internal. Yet those who think it's external will keep pursuing new people all their lives. They are attempting the "Elizabeth Taylor route to happiness"—trying out new husbands every couple of years to try to get that "up the ladder" feeling back. She gets the feeling back all right, but what she doesn't understand is that the feeling isn't caused by the new engagements. The feeling is caused by her own internal act of will, sending herself up the ladder to deal with the new person. What she doesn't understand is that she could have picked one husband and stayed with him forever if she had learned how her ladder worked and how much control she had of the ladder all along.

I was first introduced to the concept of the ladder of selves by the great British novelist and philosopher Colin Wilson. His book *Beyond the Occult* contains a much more thorough explanation of the ladder. I highly recommend his books (he's written more than 90!) because they all reveal intriguing insights about our vital reserves of power.

Colin Wilson recounts a period in his life when he had suffered from sliding down the rungs into panic attacks and had to go through the agony of his own (however brief) period of mental illness.

"I suppose that what seemed most ironic," he recalled, "was that I had always felt that I understood the cause of mental illness. A couple of years before (these panic attacks) I had written a book called *New Pathways in Psychology* in which I had argued that mental illness is basically caused by the collapse of the will. When you are making an effort, your will recharges your vital powers as a car recharges its battery when you drive it. If you cease to will, the battery goes flat, and life appears to be futile and absurd. To emerge from this state, all that is necessary is to maintain *any* kind of purposeful activity—even without much conviction—and the batteries will slowly become recharged."

Purposeful activity takes us up the ladder. Slowly at first, but up and up we go if we stay in action.

If we sit passively and dwell on our fear of other people, we send ourselves down the ladder into resentment and anger as a conditioned reflex created by habit. Then, by not engaging in any purposeful activity, our batteries will further lose their charge. We'll get that sinking *"Why even bother?"* feeling about that person.

Soon we become easy to manipulate. Because people who always relate to other people with their negative emotions are the most easily manipulated people in the world. Other reactors sense their fear, and then use their own explosive and intimidating emotions to manipulate other people.

These kinds of people who use emotions to manipulate other people are like sea cucumbers. I learned about sea cucumbers one day from Jocelyn Little who writes about weird animal facts. The sea cucumber will, if attacked, spray its attacker with its internal organs. The predator may become entangled and poisoned in the mess, while the sea cucumber rests on the sea floor. Sound familiar?

When people learn to go *up* their ladders into their minds when dealing with other people, they become impossible to manipulate and therefore can freely learn to create good relationships.

For me, the power of the ladder is in how quickly I can visualize it. Where am I on my ladder right now? I always know! And by making that knowledge conscious, I can explain to myself why I feel as I do.

#26 Be Your Commitment

Do you know the difference between involvement and commitment? Think of eggs and ham. The chicken is involved. The pig is committed.

—Martina Navratilova

I think the most often overlooked principle in relationship-building is the principle of daily renewal.

My commitments to other people will all grow weak if I never recommit to them. If I don't renew my commitment to you, the commitment must grow weaker. Whenever I have great relationships, it's because I am aware that commitment is a creation. The commitments I have to other people are created by me. If I'm clear on that, I can then move on to renewing all the commitments I want to renew each day.

Sometimes this takes only a few seconds, but it is very valuable time spent. It's a simple matter of reminding myself of my priorities and what I'm up to in life.

People who struggle with relationships don't understand the power behind renewed commitments. They think commitments are somehow external to the mind. They exist in the gut, or somewhere else. In fact, when I consult with people who are having trouble, whether they are CEOs having trouble with partners or managers or customers, or people having trouble at home with family members, the problems almost always begin with the same misunderstanding: the feeling that commitments exist independent of the person creating the commitment.

You can hear the misunderstanding in their language. They talk about commitment as if it began as something in the air, like a virus. "I'm not feeling as much commitment to my wife as I used to," they will say. I expect them to hold their stomachs, probing for the pocket of pain that went away. "I'm not feeling the same commitment to this job and this company I used to feel," some people say. To them, commitment is just a feeling.

But commitment is not a feeling. It's a decision. We can decide to make *whatever* commitment we want, to *whomever* we want, *whenever* we want. The world is divided between those who know that and those who don't know that.

Once we have made a commitment to love or serve someone it is a good idea not to put the expression of that commitment off. It's a good idea to act on that gentle commitment every day. Especially because it's so easy to do. A newspaper column by my friend Dale Dauten brought that sense of urgency home to me in a dramatic way not long ago.

Dauten recounted a meeting he had with his brilliantly eccentric friend Roger Axford (the man Dale based his main character Max on in his two wonderful books, *The Max Strategy* and *The Gifted Boss*). In that meeting, Dale had asked Axford a variation on the question of what life is all about. Axford told him to go to a hospital, any hospital, go into the chapel, and find the book where people write their thoughts about their loved ones. "There you'll find your answer," said Axford.

One day Dale took his advice and went into a hospital where he found the guest book in the chapel. He read many passages that people had written there, many prayers for loved ones in surgery, many touching thoughts written by people in states of shock and grief and hope. Among the messages written he found this one:

"Dear Lord: It's day 22. I am grateful that my son is breathing on his own. I hope you can let us have another little miracle and let him open his eyes or squeeze our hands."

Dale said that in seeing the people's passages, he found that the secret to life is that there is no secret. "It's all there," he realized, "we only need to experience it. Nine-tenths of wisdom is appreciation. Go find somebody's hand and squeeze it, while there's time."

#27 Become a Problem

The intellectual function of trouble is to lead people to think.

—John Dewey

If you have a relationship problem right now, the fastest way to solve it is to *become* the problem.

To actually say to yourself, "I am the problem," because, as was revealed in the great study of American business, *The Flight of the Buffalo*, it's only when you're willing to see yourself as the problem that you can become the solution.

If you're the problem, you're the solution. The willingness to say, " I am the problem," will take you up your ladder into pure creativity. Although most people think the opposite would happen—that you would go down your ladder into guilt, but that's not so.

Let me give you an example to show you the power—absolute power—of learning to say, "I am the problem."

Let's say I am the football coach and the players keep showing up late for team meetings. If I'm like most people, I'll waste all my energy and emotions blaming the players who show up late and trying to change them.

If my players are showing up late, the only chance I have to solve this problem is to get alone with myself and say, "I am the problem." If my players are coming in late, I am the problem, and if I am the problem, I am the solution.

So now I want to go to work figuring out what it is that I am doing that permits this problem to go on. How am I allowing it to happen? All of a sudden, I see that my rules are not strong enough and my consequences aren't creative enough. I might decide to increase the creativity of my behavior. I might make some new rules: "Meetings start at 8 in the morning. There will be no one late for the meetings, there will be no such thing as late. At 8 o'clock I'll lock the door to the meeting room. Anyone not inside has *missed* the meeting." The players know that the penalty for missing a team meeting is significant, so all of a sudden I find that the players are arriving *early* for team meetings.

Problem solved.

Notice what happened to this problem. I never said that the players weren't responsible for showing up late. Of course they were responsible. Of course they were "to blame" in a certain sense. But the more time I spent blaming them, the more time I would have wasted.

When I said, "I am the problem," I wasn't seeking to blame myself or feel guilty, I was seeking a solution. It was for intellectual leverage only. It gave me a fresh new advantage over the situation to say that I was the problem.

The function of trouble

I worked as a consultant to a company recently where a manager of a good-sized team complained to me about the nature of the meetings he led.

"Our meetings are always griping sessions," he said. "They are always about the problems in the company, and they are always dominated by the most eloquent whiners. People leave my meetings feeling depressed. The other day, one of my best workers asked me if I knew Dr. Kervorkian's phone number after one of our more depressing gripe sessions. What can I do?"

"You might want to experiment with your meetings being centered on acknowledgment," I said. "Your people might want to acknowledge each other at a certain time at the beginning of the meetings so that they realize how much they appreciate each other, and so that they can understand specifically what it is that they appreciate about each other, so that they can learn to do more of it."

"Hey, that would be great," he said, "but my problem is my people. They're all whiners."

"No, no, that's not the problem," I said.

"What do you mean?" he said.

"If I thought you could hear me, I would tell you right now what the problem is," I said.

"Hey, I can hear you. This has been the biggest problem in my life as a manager. Do you think I don't want to listen? If you think you know what the problem is, please tell me."

"You're the problem."

"Me!" he shouted. "I'm the most positive person in the company. *They're* the problem."

"Until you see that you are the problem you'll never see that you are the solution."

It wasn't long before he got the point. A few weeks after our consultation, he invited me to one of his team meetings. He stood up in front of his team and I heard him proudly address them. There was something different about his voice. It had an exciting little edge to it, the kind of edge you get when you're nervous but very happy.

"As is our new custom," he said, "we're going to begin this meeting with Wins and Acknowledgments. This is the time when we go around the room acknowledging each other for the things we've done for each other and for the company in the last week. Who wants to begin?"

I then saw about six hands go up, and he called on one person to get it started. I was amazed at how enthusiastic the team members were about praising each other.

By consciously and deliberately building Wins and Acknowledgments into his team meetings, he had changed the rules of the game. He had *become* the problem, so that he could *become* the solution. He had single-handedly altered his own team's culture and morale. He didn't have to wait for it to come from above, as most managers think they do. He didn't have to wait for his company to become perfect (a long wait) for him to start to create the meetings he always wanted to have.

This manager is like all of us. By simply not stating, "I am the problem," we all miss a golden opportunity to jump ahead into the creative problem-solving mode. There is no shame in it, because it's just a mental exercise.

The reason people don't think to try this mental trick is because of their fear of feeling guilty. People's fear of being the one to blame robs them of the life that's possible for them when they seize they joy of *becoming* all their people problems right away.

#28 Lift People Up

Celebrate what you want to see more of.

—Tom Peters

The real fun in relationship-building begins on the inside, and *then* looks outward. If I make an inner commitment to be optimistic and celebrate what's truly good about people, when I look outward, I like what I see.

The inner strength grows and grows every time I focus on what's good about someone. Soon I'm noticing how easy it is to do it.

None of that good feeling depends on the approval of other people. However, when we become optimistic, people do seem to change. Optimism becomes attractive.

The fact that other people treat us better, understand us better, and increase the behavior we are acknowledging, is a side benefit. It's only the unexpected additional pleasure. The true joy is what the optimism does for us inside.

Field Marshall Montgomery used to say that the first and foremost responsibility of a leader is optimism. If your people do not feel uplifted after their meeting with you, he declared, then you are not a leader.

This is true of parenting, too. Although most parents would rather use the devices of shaming and scaring their children into doing things, because it's so much easier and faster, it is always better leadership to take the time to generate optimism.

Every situation or problem has an upside and a downside. Every thing we talk to our kids or spouse or team members at work about has an upside and a downside. To focus on the downside is the easiest thing to do. To judge and be critical takes only the smallest portion of the brain to pull off.

What takes the biggest use of the brain is vision. To engage both the left side (logical, linear) of the brain and the right side (creative, visionary) of the brain takes more time and energy and courage. But the rewards are enormous. Optimism pays off in big ways in human communications.

If I am going to be transferred by my company to another city, the easiest and laziest way to communicate that to my family is quickly, carelessly, and pessimistically.

"Hi hon, hi kids," I say in a worn-down victim's voice of someone who has been swamped and overwhelmed by yet another day of unfairness at work.

"Hey, you guys, come here, I've got to tell you something," I say in a voice that portends some bad news. "Um, I don't know how to put this but I got word today that I'm being transferred. Yeah. We're going to have to move. It won't be for another month or two, and they haven't explained everything to me yet. They never do. But we're going to have to move."

What I've told my family is the "truth" in a way. But it is not the whole truth. It's just the worst part of the news. It's the easiest way to communicate with them because it takes no imagination or foresight. But it is a shame to do it this way, because I have missed an opportunity to show them what's good about the move. There is no chance that they can be uplifted by the news, and therefore I am not demonstrating any leadership.

Optimism becomes contagious

And by "optimism" I'm not referring to the frothy kind of "positive thinking" that leads people to become irrational. I'm not talking about becoming that obnoxious kind of happy camper who will not listen to other people's troubles—the shallow papering over of reality with empty and nice thoughts. I'm talking about true optimism. Seeing the true and real *up*side of each situation and then emphasizing it because it *is* true and real.

I would create better relationships with my family if I developed a habit of being more optimistic. If I took my time and researched everything I could about the new state we were moving to, I could have the meeting focused on that. If I researched beautiful neighborhoods and good schools I was looking at, I could talk a lot about that. If I researched all the good aspects of my new position after the transfer, I could talk a lot about that. Every situation has good things about it and bad things. The easiest thing is to focus on the bad. To complain. But that's not leadership and that doesn't create good relationships.

#29 Act the Part

The real secret of success is enthusiasm. Yes, more than enthusiasm, I would say excitement. I like to see people get excited. When they get excited they make a success of their lives.

—Walter Chrysler

The great American philosopher Emmet Fox once uncovered something very profound when he said, "Love acts the part."

It took me a long time to really let that sink in. Love acts like love would act. It doesn't act some other part.

Sometimes we try to change someone's personality, or stifle their creativity in the name of love. For centuries in our culture, as an example, men did not grant women the same freedoms they granted themselves. They often ridiculed women and held them back. In a remarkable letter to his brother written in the 1940s, the novelist John O'Hara showed the beginnings of a larger shift in attitude when he wrote,

"Here is the only piece of straight advice: Never forget that your girl or your wife is every damn bit as much a person as you are....She thinks the world revolves around her just as you do around yourself, just as anyone does. She has a vote in life as well as in politics, she eats and sleeps and suffers and loves and thinks....like you and me. She was born, she lives, she's got to die; and for you to attempt to dominate her, to pinch her personality, is some kind of sin."

#30 Build the Love In

A man without a smile should not open a shop.

—Chinese Proverb

Love operates in the universe in a very mathematical way.

Whatever gets put in to one side of the equation shows up on the other. Maybe not right away and maybe not in the same place you put it, but the love always comes back. People who have great relationships in life have a relationship to the idea of love that's very active. They experience love as something they can create. Something that they can build into their lives to whatever degree they wish.

People who struggle in relationships have the opposite concept of love. They see love as being "out there somewhere." They always talk about love as coming *into* their lives. They wait for love and they hope they'll get lucky.

Some even believe in a mythological cupid—a flying chubby baby armed with a bow and arrow who may or may not choose to shoot them full of love.

I know a woman who's jealous of her sister because her sister seems to be "lucky in love." This woman wishes that *she* were so lucky and believes life has been unfair to her so far. "My sister is very, very lucky," she says. "She had someone special come into her life at just the right time. I wish someone like that could come into my life. I have so much to give to someone if they would come into my life."

Love doesn't simply come into one's life. It must first go out. It must go out bravely and without guarantee. It then circles around awhile so that you'll see no connection. Finally it comes back in. That's the only way it travels and materializes. By going out into the world, connecting with someone else, and, later, coming right back to you, multiplied.

#31 Do the Thing

*The greater part of courage is
having done it before.
Do the thing, and you shall have the power.*

—Ralph Waldo Emerson

Let's say I'm back in high school and I have a crush on you.

Let's say I think you are beautiful (or as my kids would put it, let's say I think you're hot). I might be nervous about talking to you, and I'd certainly be nervous about asking you out. In fact, knowing my past history, I would be frozen with fear.

But the reason I'm afraid to ask you out is usually not due to some deep psychological defect I have to work on. It's simply because I've never asked someone like you out. So it's like Emerson said: If I had done it before I'd have more courage now.

But it feels like the reason I haven't done it before is because I have not *found* the courage. It feels like there's something missing inside of me. And until that certain something is there, I am helpless.

So which comes first, the courage to act, or the act?

Most people believe you have to have the courage first. You have to have it in you somewhere. But that's not really true. And in fact, *thinking* that it's true limits people and prevents the enjoyment of other people.

Because the truth is what Emerson says it is: *The act itself* must come first. First the action, then the courage. Do the thing you are afraid of and the fear will eventually diminish. *Do the thing and you shall have the power.*

But the reason I don't do the thing is because I don't think I have the power to do it. I've talked myself out of action. So I've talked myself out of my own dreams.

I work with a lot of salespeople who are constantly battling various fears. This is because selling is now the great heroic adventure of our age. In a globally competitive free enterprise system, salespeople are the hunters and warriors of today. They are our pathfinders and deerslayers.

And, therefore, they face fear daily: fear of cold-calling, fear of meeting with powerful decision-makers, fear of closing a business deal, fear of making a really large request of someone. And because salespeople are just people, their fears are our fears. There is no real separation between salespeople and other average people. In fact, as Robert Louis Stevenson said, "Everyone lives by selling something."

I've known salespeople who go into psychotherapy—attend weekend consciousness-raising retreats and do all sorts of things to decrease their fear, so that they'll have the courage to do the thing they are afraid to do. But I've never seen anything work as fast or cause so much joy as simply doing it.

Action comes first and courage hurries to catch up with it. Don't wait until you have the courage to act, because courage is flirtatious. It will wait even longer than you do. What it's waiting for is you. It will activate when *you* do.

Just *make* the call. Just *close* the sale. Just *ask* her out. Do the thing, and you shall have the power.

#32 Try to Understand

Living is easy with eyes closed,
misunderstanding all you see.

—John Lennon

We only fear what we don't understand.

And the more we learn about what we don't understand, the more we realize that knowledge is power. Not power over the other person, but power over our consciousness. Power to relate to someone in a confident and comfortable way.

Many times, our habit is to worry about other people. A habit, by the way, that takes us right out of the possibility of creative thinking.

The people who create the best relationships are the people who think the most creatively about other people. The people who have the worst relationships are the people who worry the most about other people. Horace Walpole once made an observation about this side of human nature: "The world is a comedy for those who think and a tragedy for those who feel."

It's easier not to understand someone else. To just go with our gut feelings about them, our gut suspicions. Living is easy with eyes closed.

But great friendships and great professional connections are always made through understanding the other person. Taking an interest. Becoming a thinker and an expert on that person. Eyes wide open. That's what works. We only fear what we don't understand.

Misunderstanding all we see

"What does fear have to do with it?" the manager of a team of telecommunications workers asked me. "I just flat out don't like this customer. Never have. Never will."

"At the heart of all emotions are two basic emotions," I said, "fear and love. You can trace any negative feeling to fear. You can trace any positive feeling to love. Those are the two roots of all feelings. If you hate someone, that means you're afraid of something. If you're mad at someone you're afraid of losing something."

"What if someone cuts me off in traffic?" he asked. "I flip him off and yell. I'm not afraid, in fact I want to pull the guy from his car and confront him. I'm not afraid. I'm not afraid of anybody."

"Perhaps not in the macho sense, if you think like Jackie Chan thinks. But you are afraid of *something*. To be angry, you have to be. In traffic you're afraid that the other person's driving is a threat; they could cause an accident. You're afraid of that. If you weren't afraid, you wouldn't be angry. It's as simple as that. You can trace any anger you have to a fear."

"So I don't get what you're saying here. I don't think I feel fear when I get enraged in traffic."

"Do you ever play those video games where you drive in a race or something?" I asked him.

"Oh, sure. I like those."

"When a car cuts you off in those games, do you get angry at them and become enraged?"

"No, of course not. They're just images on a screen. I yell a lot and have fun and get frustrated. But I don't feel any rage."

"That's because you have nothing to be afraid of. You said it yourself—they're just images on a screen. They can't hurt you. If they can't hurt you, you can't feel rage. It won't be there. Rage is based on fear."

"Okay, maybe in real-life traffic I'm afraid I'll get in an accident, or lose my composure. I like to think when I drive. Maybe just being rudely cut off causes fear of loss of safety."

"That's right! If you're angry, you're afraid of losing something. Now you see it."

"So the solution is to understand?"

"Exactly."

"What if I don't want to understand?"

"Then don't. That's fine."

"Because when I'm driving or something, I think it's healthy to be ticked off once in awhile. It keeps me alert."

"Fine. If it serves you, use it. Feelings are not the enemy."

"Okay, I see. But still I don't think my hatred of this one customer serves me. I don't like it, and it takes up a lot of time and it can ruin a good day."

"I would agree with that."

"So you're saying to understand him."

"...and the fear will go away. When the fear goes away, the anger will go away. It has to. All anger comes from fear and we only fear what we don't understand. You still might not like him, if he's mean or unreasonable, but you don't have to feel all that anger about it. The anger means there's fear somewhere. Fear that he'll ruin your good day. Or fear based on your past...he might have the voice of someone who gave you a lot of pain as a child. It doesn't really matter where the fear comes from. Once you understand him you won't fear him. We only fear what we don't understand."

"Yeah, yeah, you keep saying that."

"Because it's true, and it's the key."

"Maybe if I learned more about this customer. Maybe if I paid him a visit and found out what his world was like, what *he* was afraid of. What his dreams were."

"Now you've got it," I said. "You don't need me anymore. You know exactly how to do this."

#33 Don't Take a Person Personally

No one can make me feel inferior without my permission.

—Eleanor Roosevelt

I work with a lot of companies who pride themselves on being able to hire good customer-relations people. As I've worked with these companies, I've found that there's one characteristic that most distinguishes a great customer relations person—they don't take customers personally.

Does that mean they don't care? No. It just means that they don't take customers personally. Therefore, they can have more fun with them—even the angry customers.

The people who have a hard time in customer relations are in the habit of reacting to customers emotionally. Angry customers really push their buttons, and they get frustrated and upset, and then try to defend their company. In the end, they're undone by their own defensiveness.

And keep in mind—it's just a habit to be so afraid of other people that you choose emotional reactions to them all the time, and wear yourself out trying to satisfy them. Great customer relations people don't mind an angry customer because they use the anger as a signal to go up their ladders into their minds. They get creative and they get clever. They get thoughtful and they get strategic. They take it as an intellectual challenge—not a personal emotional challenge.

"I think I'm Meryl Streep," a woman from an office supply company in Las Vegas told me. "I'm an actress. My whole approach with customers is to pretend that I am on their side all the way. To act the part of a total customer advocate. When they're upset, I encourage them to get even more upset. When they're through talking, I ask them to tell me more. I suggest that this must have affected them in more ways than they've already told me. When I'm absolutely convinced that they have said everything that's on their minds and then some, and that I've given them every great acting expression in the world to let them know that I'm with them all the way...including always mirroring their body movements, their hand gestures, their voice tones, and facial expressions...then I tell them I am on their side. I tell them that I am going to do everything in my power to make things right for them. I convince them that it's them and me against the whole corporate structure, but we will do it. We are not afraid. When it comes time to ask them specifically what kind of amends we should get the company to make for them, an amazing thing happens. They are no longer so angry. Some of them tell me, '*You've already done it. All I wanted was someone who cared...someone who would listen to me. You've done that.*'"

This woman's manager told me that she got the best customer reviews of all her employees and *also had to give out the fewest refunds.*

It's a wonderful example of the power of the mind. To make a game out of it, to be like Meryl Streep and *act as if* you are totally compassionate and empathetic gets you even better results than waiting for your feelings to tell you what to do. Most people who struggle with customer relations struggle because they make it a carry-over from all their unsatisfying personal relationships in the past. A continuation of the struggle to be validated. When what it really *could* be is a whole new beginning. A chance to relate from the future instead of from the past.

#34 Celebrate Your Independence

*Hating someone is like burning your
house down to get rid of a rat.*

—Harry Emerson Fosdick

One of the most secure states of mind you can be in for creating relationships is a state that was taught to me by hypnotherapist Lindsay Brady. Brady's term for this state is *emotional independence.*

When I'm emotionally independent, I don't let my emotions depend on how other people treat me or what other people say to me. My emotions are mine to cultivate and nurture and I'm not about to give that secure sense of control away.

My emotions are feelings I get from the thought patterns I construct in my head. When I respond to a customer who is shouting at me by getting scared and then angry it is only a habit. Is it the habit I want? Does it serve me?

If I would rather form a more secure-feeling habit than that, I can. I might start by choosing to become *more* conscious—not less—when the customer is angry. I might rather go *up* my ladder of consciousness than *down*. And I know that either direction can be made into a habit. So I might rather train myself to respond thoughtfully, even cleverly, in the face of someone's anger instead of emotionally, or frozenly.

People used to believe that their emotions were all caused by outside events and other people. (People also used to believe that the world was flat.)

People who still believe in what psychologist Dr. William Glasser calls the "stimulus/response view of the world" are making a mistake that is even greater than believing that the world is flat. By believing that you have no choice but to just *respond* to whatever stimulus is out there, you've surrendered all the power within you to create a life.

People do not have the absolute power to scare us. People do not have the capacity to make us mad. People don't intimidate us, and people don't frustrate or irritate us. It just *seems* like they do—in the same hallucinatory false way that the world *seems* like it's flat. Fortunately we know better about the world, but most of us don't know better about other people. By imagining that other people are the problem, we extend the hallucination into a futility by then trying to change other people. The way we know this is dysfunctional thinking based on mistaken beliefs, is that it never works.

There's only one process that works. That process is creative thinking followed by courageous action. The exciting conclusion we reach after enough practice is this: We *create* the relationships in our lives by what *we* think and the actions *we* take.

Relationships are best created when they don't feel out of control. Control is the source of that great feeling in a relationship when both sides are enjoying every challenge. Not control in the false sense of controlling another person, but control in the true sense of controlling our own consciousness.

But it just doesn't matter

My friend Carson suffered a very dramatic breakup with a man with whom she had been living in Michigan for seven years. She had watched as he allowed himself to be seduced by a woman who hung out in health clubs and looked for people to seduce. It wasn't a simple case of bad judgment, or a "mistake" (as our top statesmen like to call it when they are caught violating their marriages). It was a betrayal. And it had been coming on for years.

Carson took a while to grieve the loss of the relationship after bravely throwing her man out of her life. That grieving process was going to have to occur, whether she liked it or not. She was like a lioness with a thorn in her paw. It would have to work its way out on its own.

But Carson also knew that there were things she could do to eventually achieve emotional independence from the whole affair. She knew that emotions live in the body and are experienced in the body. ("Feelings are felt," she said.) She learned that when the body is broken down, as it is when we have the flu, we are in less emotional control than usual. Conversely, when the body is built up, negative emotions have a harder time fastening onto anything. In a body singing with oxygen, negative emotions feel out of place.

So Carson went on a program of aerobics and dance. She worked out every day, pumping her lungs full of life-giving oxygen, and expanding her consciousness in ever-widening arcs (as every aerobic activity will do).

She signed up for a musical chorus and began meeting new people and taking part in concerts being performed around the community.

She declared herself to be starting a new life. She identified the personal betrayal as the end of the chapter that was Part One in the book of her life. By thinking of it that way, the betrayal even began to take on some positive qualities. The qualities of a turning point.

Every day her emotional independence grew. She went through an angry period, where she was just flat-out furious with her partner for what he had done. She was also angry with herself for letting such an obviously uncommitted relationship last for so long. But soon the anger gave way to an intoxicating new feeling: the feeling of not really caring.

"I remember the day I woke up and realized I no longer cared," she said. "I no longer cared about him or who he was seeing or what he was doing. It just didn't matter."

When my children were young, I used to use a scene from Bill Murray's wonderful little movie *Meatballs*. My kids especially loved the part in the movie when it's a day after the first day of the two-day camp olympics between Murray's camp of regular kids and the opposing camp across the lake of rich kids. The rich kids were way ahead in the competition and Murray's character calls a meeting of all the kids in his camp the night before the final day of competition. As he announces each and every advantage the rich kids have in life over his kids he gets an insane look on his face and yells, "But it doesn't matter! It just doesn't matter!" Soon all the of kids are shouting, "It just doesn't matter, it just doesn't matter!"

My kids loved that movie and we watched it more times than I can count. And we also developed the habit, when life threw our family one kind of minor tragedy after another, of gathering ourselves together and having one of us spell out each one of the things about the tragedy we didn't like, and after saying it, yelling, "but it doesn't matter." And finally, when all of the bad things were brought out into the open all of us would march around the house, just like in the movie, shouting at the top of our lungs, "it just doesn't matter, it just doesn't *matter!*"

Consciousness is like a flashlight in a storm. It shows the way out of emotional entanglements. The first step is to ask myself the question: Where will I shine my light?

If I shine it on how I can serve someone in life, then I can really enjoy the feeling of new control. As long as I am making a difference, I am in control of my light. I am in control of my imagination and the energy of my thoughts.

But the minute my attention slips out of my control and starts roving free, seeking out little painful feelings in my system, I begin to worry. I begin to wonder what you think of me and why. I have lost my independence.

The way back is this: My emotions are mine, not other people's. They are valuable and full of fresh color and energy. I will practice every day working with them and keeping them independent of other people. Every day will become independence day.

#35 Make a Difference

Your life's meaning is the difference that it makes. If it doesn't make a difference, it has no meaning.

—Lyndon Duke

At one time in my life my professional relationships weren't what I wanted them to be, so I enlisted the help of consultant Lyndon Duke.

Although Lyndon's lifelong research was on the linguistics of suicide, he discovered during his studies that if you can understand suicide, you can understand all human unhappiness. It's just a matter of degree.

Soon he became a consultant to a wide spectrum of professional people who wanted to learn his ideas. If those ideas could stop a suicide, they could also stop all the unpleasant states that fall short of that act. His focus was on showing people how to have a life that meant something.

"Meaning is nothing more than the difference it makes," he told me. "If it doesn't make a difference, it has no meaning. When you are on your death bed, what you will be asking yourself is, What's different? What is different on this planet because I was here? If nothing is different, then you didn't make a difference. If you didn't make a difference, your life had no meaning. That's all meaning is—the difference it makes. What doesn't make a difference has no meaning."

I visited Lyndon where he lives in Oregon to learn his ideas. He told me his life story, and it was very similar to my own, with one exception: He began his adult life as an exceptionally successful man. He was a scholar and a respected professor. But he experienced a very serious bottoming-out after awhile and remembered lying face down on his carpet in total despair. He didn't know how to go on. Then, as he was lying there, he heard a sound. It was his next door neighbor mowing the lawn. And above the sound of the mower he heard singing. His neighbor was singing while he was mowing his lawn, and it hit Lyndon like a light— that's what I want! More than anything! To have a life that simple and happy that I can mow the lawn and feel like singing at the same time.

He wanted that. That was his new desire: to be an average person enjoying life in a simple way.

Lyndon explained that he realized that one's lifelong desire doesn't have to be for anything exceptional. It can be for a very simple form of comfort and joy. It can be for the pleasure of singing while performing a chore.

Lyndon was an extraordinary intellect who wanted to make that fact irrelevant to his happiness. He knew he had a lot of work to do to get to the simple pleasure of being an "average person," but he was excited by the idea of trying.

As he sat telling me about his journey to happiness, he was speaking with a very excited voice. It was clear that he was now a very happy man who wanted to make a difference by sharing how he got that way.

"Happiness and a meaningful life come from making differences. But this is the most important rule to follow: Always make the differences you *can* make," he said, "not the differences you would prefer to make but can't. As you keep making differences, your skill will automatically and effortlessly increase. Anything human beings repeat they get more skillful at. Including misery!"

When he said, "Including misery!" he let go with a huge long laugh. That was his fun—exposing human folly and showing the way to avoid it.

Society pushes exceptionality

After my weekend with Lyndon, I flew back home to Arizona with my head full of wonderful ideas. Already I had begun to apply them. Rather than always trying to be exceptional at everything, I discovered I could be happy with simply being an average person doing what I could do to make a difference. This took so much pressure off. Because trying to be exceptional was wearing me out and I was never satisfied. I was never exceptional enough, to begin with. And sometimes being exceptional took so much energy that I had to take time off to just crash and be depressed for a while until I couldn't stand myself any longer and it was time to go out and try to be exceptional again.

The other problem with holding myself to the standard of being exceptional was that I often couldn't do it at all, and I got so discouraged, I would do nothing. And doing nothing is less than what an average person does.

The final downside to trying to be exceptional was how it distanced me from other people. Average people are not comfortable being around self-described exceptional people. Exceptional people, by definition, are isolated from others. They don't relate well. They are the exceptions.

Lyndon taught me to keep repeating my average day, and things would get better on their own. Anything repeated gets better. By small comfortable increments. None of the white-knuckled striving and jamming and forcing my way to the top of the heap. Just a happy average person having a happy average day. I was so pleased with how well this low-pressure approach was working for me, I even began mystifying my friends by signing my messages, "have an average day."

I had realized that always telling myself to have a "great" day was putting a lot of pressure on. Telling myself that either I had to be exceptional or I wasn't worth anything was disconnecting me from the human family. Lyndon Duke had discovered how this kind of pressure led to suicide. The pressure to be exceptional. He had also discovered that when potential suicides learned to allow themselves to be average, the pressure was released and people could live again and experience the happiness of daily small improvements.

"All of society pushes exceptionality on us," Lyndon said. "Parents, especially, think it is their duty to urge their children to be exceptional. They don't know the harm it does."

I couldn't wait for my next meeting with Lyndon, which was to be the following weekend. I flew up from Arizona to Oregon and he met me at the airport to take me to my hotel. Our studies would begin again bright and early the next morning.

As I ate breakfast in the hotel dining room that next morning, a very strange thing happened. A rumpled, ruddy little man in an undersized hotel uniform burst into the restaurant calling out my name. I looked up and identified myself and he said, with fear on his face, "You have an emergency phone call at the front desk!"

My heart pounded as I left with him, wondering if my children were okay. When I got to the phone it was a nurse on the line who said she was from a hospital in Eugene. She was talking about Lyndon.

"He's had a heart attack. We think he has a hole in his aorta. He had severe heart pains early this morning and we rushed him here. He has to have an emergency operation, and he's in very critical condition."

I was stunned. Lyndon had been so buoyant and full of life the evening before at the airport. I remembered how happy he was to hear about how average my previous week had been.

"How critical is critical?" I asked. "How serious is this? Can I see him?"

"No you can't see him now. And this is very critical; there are no guarantees here. But I did want to call you because he insisted. It was one of the most unusual things I've ever seen. He not only insisted that I call you, but he also begged me to let him give his lessons to you. He wanted us to let him teach you while we were prepping him for this operation. I told him it was out of the question, but he kept insisting! I finally had to tell him once again that he'd had a potentially fatal heart attack and we were trying to save his life! First things first!"

"That's just like him," I said.

"What?"

"He lives for the differences he can make. He's been making a big difference in my life. He wanted to continue. That's all. Please save him."

"Please what?" she said as static came on the line.

"Please save his life," I said more clearly, pushing the words past the lump in my throat.

"Yes," she said. "We're going to do what we can."

I walked back to the restaurant in a sad state of shock. I gathered my books and notebook and walked slowly back to my room.

Although his recovery was complicated by a stroke suffered during surgery, Lyndon surprised everyone by fighting back and working to get his life of difference-making back. Soon he was out of the hospital and living with his daughter to continue his rehabilitation. The doctors were amazed that he had suffered so much and still made it through.

I was not amazed.

On the street where you live

There is a little old man in my neighborhood that I see out walking every morning. He walks slowly, with a slight limp (almost as if he's had a knee or hip replacement) and he's always cheerful when he sees people.

But if you watch him on his walk, as I do almost every morning as I get into my car, you notice something. Every time he finds a morning newspaper on the sidewalk, in the street, in a driveway or on a lawn he always picks it up and carriers it up to the front porch of the home that it belongs to. He does this all morning, all along the street, with every house he passes. He picks up people's papers and puts them on the front porch for them.

I used to watch him before I met Lyndon, wondering why he did that. But after Lyndon's teaching, I understood. This was difference-making on display for me. It was difference-making at its most basic. Something is always different because of this man. With every house he passes, something is different than it was before.

Before he arrives, there is a paper out there someplace, in the street, on the lawn, wherever. A hassle. And after he passes, it is now conveniently located on the front porch. That's a difference.

This man is a true difference-maker. This might not be the difference he would *prefer* to make. If he were an exceptionality freak, he'd probably be drunk and depressed because he had not been able to make a bigger difference in people's lives. But this was the difference he was easily *able* to make. Lyndon's words come back to me every time I see this little morning man: "Focus on the differences you *can* make, not the differences you would prefer to make but can't."

#**36** Reveal Yourself

I do not ask how the wounded one feels.
I, myself, become the wounded one.

—Walt Whitman, Leaves of Grass

My friend Jim Blasingame and I were trying to make an appointment to talk on the phone in a week or so and because he lives down south and I live in Arizona, we were struggling to get the time zones right.

His time was Central Time and my time was Mountain Time, and because Mountain never changes and because Central was about to go on daylight savings, I was hopelessly frustrated trying to figure out what time was what.

My wife, Kathy, just happens to be quite good at figuring things out that confuse me, (like directions, map-reading, checking accounts, and so on) so I asked her for help by e-mail:

Kathy:

> If I'm doing a long distance phone conference next week at 7 Central, and the time changes this weekend, what time will it be Mountain? I am totally confused about this and Blasingame is helpless in the face of this, too. Men can't do this.

Kathy wrote back to me that she uses the little formula called "spring ahead, fall behind" to calculate the effect of daylight savings on Mountain Time, and it's a formula that makes this more mystifying than ever to me because I have no idea what that formula does. (Do you spring yourself or the other zone ahead?) However she did it, Kathy calculated the correct Mountain time for the conversation to be at 5 a.m. for me. Rather than create a whole new communication, I simply forwarded the whole e-mail exchange to Jim.

Apparently, that was a mistake. Because here was Jim's reply to me, after having seen my message that "Blasingame is helpless in the face of this, too. Men can't do this."

"Steve, Stever, Steverinsky, Steve-man—never, never, ever admit weakness to women. (Unless, of course, you're working that sensitive angle to get lucky.) We have so few secrets, and women have all those mystique, mystery, secret things they scam us with. I had no idea you were going to blow our cover. Besides, the problem is not guys' math skills, it's you damn contrary Arizonans refusing to go on daylight savings time. What's up with that?!"

I could see that this was a totally facetious e-mail. Jim likes to have fun. He hosts a nationwide radio show called The Small Business Advocate and he plays Allman Brothers music on his show and generally takes the seriousness out of business and puts the fun back in.

But in his teasingly mock-sexist e-mail, something occurred to me. (So often, humor seems to contain a real truth.) He said we should never reveal our weaknesses to women unless we are going to work that angle to "get lucky." I think we know what Jim meant by getting lucky. But let's look deeper.

When you hear one person talking about a marital relationship that has been successful and for which they are grateful, they will usually say, "I am a very lucky man." Or, "My first marriage didn't work out, but this time it has. I feel very lucky." These are longer-lasting and even better kinds of "lucky" than Jim was referring to, but the access to them might be the same.

I began to see a clue as to where those lucky relationships come from, and in Jim's humor I saw the clue. When we are willing to reveal weaknesses, we tend to get lucky. When we drop all pretense of being superhuman and confess to being afraid, or confused, or jealous, or whatever, we somehow grow closer to the person we are confessing to, and that person grows closer to us.

We get lucky when we reveal ourselves.

Becoming the wounded one

I have a friend named Darby who was wondering how to respond to his young son one day when the boy came home from school after being terrorized by bullies on the playground. Darby decided to tell his son a story of how he himself had been frightened and humiliated by bullies when he was little. One of them actually held Darby down and forced clumps of dirt and grass into Darby's mouth. Today, Darby is a tall and imposing confident motivational speaker. To picture him as a terrified little boy with dirt being forced into his mouth must have been very dramatic for his son.

"I wanted him to know that he wasn't alone," Darby said. "I wanted him to realize that there was nothing wrong with him, and that he wasn't a coward."

After establishing that deeply compassionate connection, Darby and his son could talk about the action they were going to take to see that the bullying didn't happen again.

What Darby did to create closeness with his son was to reveal his own weakness and his own humanity. Contrast that to what many other people would do in a similar situation.

"You shouldn't feel afraid!" they would yell. "You should report those boys! You should stand up to them! You don't have anything to be afraid about. Why are you so afraid?"

When people are uncomfortable with another person's feelings, the first impulse is to make those feelings wrong. To tell them that they shouldn't be feeling that way. But that kind of communication only causes distance. Whenever we make someone wrong for how they're feeling, we put distance between us.

It is helpful to have the awareness that no feeling is wrong. All feelings are right. All feelings are exactly correct, because they are exactly what that person is feeling. There is no right or wrong involved. The feeling is a sensation being felt, just like a fever.

We would never say, "You shouldn't have a fever! It's wrong for you to have a fever! You have nothing to base that fever on!"

Feelings are the same thing as a fever. They are experienced in the body the same way. But we're always trying to make other peoples' feelings wrong, and, when we do, it *always* creates distance between us.

Closeness comes from revealing ourselves. It comes from dramatizing what we have in common.

#37 Take Your Time

There is no such thing as constructive criticism.

—Dale Carnegie

When a monthly women's magazine recently called to talk to me for an article they were writing on "How To Give Criticism Without Feeling Guilty," my impulse was to simply say, "You can't."

My first temptation was to say to them that you always feel guilty after criticizing somebody, and well you *should*.

In fact, there's a good reason for feeling guilty after giving criticism. Criticizing is a very unkind thing to do to someone. If your body and emotions are causing guilt to occur, that's because they are only trying to protect you from eventually losing *all* your friends. The body sends that guilt signal because the body knows you need friends to survive.

But then after talking to the nice lady from the magazine for a while I finally agreed with her point that there were *some* circumstances that would come up in a person's life when criticism was appropriate (although, it sounded like her article was going to suggest that we have to give criticism all day, every day), and if it's appropriate then why should we have to feel guilty? The answer is: We don't.

So my ultimate answer was, if you have to deliver criticism, make sure you take your time.

The most important thing about criticism is not how it is said but how it is heard. How people are hearing you is more important than what you are saying.

Take your time to talk about what your fundamental commitment is to that person. If he is your employee, and you must correct some behavior, tell him first what your primary commitment is. You are committed to his success. You are committed to his career progress. You are committed to his happiness and fulfillment on the job. You acknowledge all the good he has done and what his potential is.

Then you relate your own past to his behavior. You let him know that you consider yourself to be human like he is. You've made bigger, more embarrassing mistakes in your life than he ever will. He is no worse than you once were.

Then you point out the behavior that is working against your helping him reach his goals. You highlight the behavior that goes against the fundamental agreement you have with each other, whatever that agreement is.

Finally, you make a request. You don't criticize, or judge him, or make him wrong; you make a request. A simple request. If he agrees to fulfill your request, you have a new agreement. Agreements are mutual, they are not one person lording it over another.

Turning criticism into agreement

Many years ago, I ran a small company. We had weekly employee meetings and a woman I will call Cleo was always showing up late to our team meetings. She would come rushing in, arms full of clutter, about 10 minutes after the meeting started, with hushed apologies all around. When it came time for her to say something in the meeting, she always first mentioned her tardiness. She apologized to everyone for being late.

It was always something. Her daughter's teacher called. A client had kept her on the phone. She had to rush over to put out some business fire somewhere. There were always "good" reasons.

Finally I asked Cleo if she would meet with me. I applied my "take your time" formula. I started the conversation by telling her how much I valued her work, and how committed I was to making sure her career was succeeding. I mentioned some great things she had done, and I mentioned a few things she and I had done that had advanced her career. Then I said I was going to talk about being late to meetings, because I knew it was a source of discomfort and embarrassment to her to have it happen so often. I talked about earlier in my life, when I was always late. I had cultivated a kind of legend around being energetic, creative, and completely disorganized. The disorganized part affected my professional relationships, but somehow I couldn't figure out how to time my life so that nothing would come up to keep me from being on time.

"I finally realized that it was immaturity," I told Cleo. "I don't know if this fits for you, but being late everywhere was my final stand against growing up. I would show the world who was in control. Not the boring grown-up world that wants me to be places on time. No! I myself was in charge of my life! I would suffer any embarrassment I could to keep that illusion of control."

"But I actually do want to be on time," said Cleo.

"I don't believe that's really true," I said. "Because if you really wanted to, you would."

"No, it's just circumstances," she said. "They keep coming up at the wrong time. There's nothing I can do."

"Let's see if that's really true," I said, smiling, and she could tell that I had one of my annoying brain puzzles ready to present to her.

"Here's a question for you," I said. "Do you miss any airplanes? What I mean by that is, do you schedule flights and then not make the flight? Does that happen quite often?"

"No."

"Well, I wonder why not. I mean, all these circumstances that are preventing you from coming to our team meetings on time, they are still in operation when you have to catch a plane, right? Outside circumstances don't lose their power or stop occurring just because you've bought a plane ticket, right?"

"I guess not."

"Then why don't you miss those flights?"

"Well, I guess because flights cost a lot of money."

"Yes," I said. "That's part of it. And because they cost a lot of money, you have made them more of a priority. You've made them important to yourself and to others. In fact, I'd be willing to bet that you speak differently about them than you do about your other time commitments."

"No," she said. "Not that I'm aware of."

"I bet you do," I smiled, trying to encourage her to see the humor in this conversation. "When you've booked a flight to Chicago for next week, I bet you speak of it with the language of absolute commitment. I bet you say things like, 'I'll be in Chicago next week.' Or, 'I can't do that, I'm going to be in Chicago.' Or someone might ask you what you're doing next Wednesday at noon and you might say, 'At noon Wednesday? I'll be on a plane to Chicago.' You are speaking the language of absolute certainty."

"Okay," she said, "I guess I do talk that way about planes and flights and things like that."

"And that's because you have made them important enough in your mind to speak about them differently, and think about them differently. Because you take on the language and thoughts of absolute certainty, you never miss any flights. If a circumstance comes up, you handle it, or get someone else to."

"And you think I could do that with meetings, too?" she said.

"If you gave your word that you would, I'd bet my house that you would."

"What about traffic? What if I'm slowed up by a traffic jam?" she said.

"The best way to make certain you're not late for a meeting is not to just barely be on time, but to be early. People who are early are never late. Don't you always get to the airport a little early?"

"Yes, I do."

"So I have a request," I said. "I am requesting that you treat our team meetings with as much importance as you treat your travel plans. I am requesting that you arrive early at every team meeting for the next six weeks, and just to show me that you're keeping the agreement, I would like you to come see me at least 15 minutes before each team meeting. We can have a good talk, so your time won't be wasted. After the six weeks, I trust you completely to make it to every team meeting on time and set the standard for other people. You will do it because it represents your word, and your word is everything to you. Are you willing to do that? Don't just say yes, tell me if you are willing to make it a formal agreement."

"Okay," she said, smiling and reaching her hand out to shake mine, "I agree."

She left looking cheerful, and we never had another problem with her again showing up late to team meetings. Often I would acknowledge her to the rest of the team for being someone who kept her agreements and someone I could count on.

So, if I *must* criticize someone, it helps to take my time. Take the time to set things up. This is the process that always seems to work:

1. State my commitments to the person.

2. Relate personally to the problem by revealing my own weaknesses.

3. Make a request.

4. Seek an agreement.

Agreements are mutual, and criticism is one-sided. Criticism creates distance between us. Agreements bring us closer.

#38 Live Your Life Forward

Why don't we have a psychology that asks,
How do you change your marriage from okay back to great?
Or that advises you when your job doesn't give you joy?

—E. Martin Seligman

Some of us go back over the past too much. We never got all our resentment out about tiny past hurts and problems, so we carry them around. We work them into the next encounter with the next person we see.

But we contaminate our relationships this way.

The great philosopher Soren Kierkegarrd once said, "Philosophy is perfectly right in saying that life must be understood backward. But then one forgets the other clause—that it must be lived forward."

The same is true of relationships. They are best understood backward. They're best understood looking back throughout the history of the relationship. All those conversations we had are there to learn from. In them, people tell us, if we pay attention, how they want to be treated.

But to really grow a relationship into something fun and wonderful, whether in business or in life, the trick is to live it forward. The trick is to always picture what you want and live into that picture with every conversation, every small gift, every acknowledgment, and every act of service.

The experience is one of living forward into an intention.

When we get dragged by our emotions into the past, the trick is to gently return to what it is you *want*, the way a transcendental meditator quietly brings his attention back to a mantra. Make a mantra (a repeated thought) of your intention. Bring your attention back to it. Don't let your attention become a rolling stone, a wandering star, or a spoiled child running wild in the grocery store.

Often what people want is simpler and easier to get than they realize. The things they desire are often hidden right behind the next door. Once, a company in Phoenix, Ariz., showed me internal surveys that revealed that some of their employees thought the company "lacked the courage and the will" to properly measure and manage each others' performance. I suggested that they did not lack the courage and the will (because no human really lacks these things). I asked them to consider the possibility that all they lacked was a routine.

Sometimes when I think I lack willpower all I really lack is a routine. If I want to lose weight, the easy thing to tell myself is that I lack the will to exercise. But that's not really the truth. All I lack is a routine.

Figure out what you want and begin a simple routine that makes certain you do something about it every day. Pay attention to your intention and it will become reality.

If I want a friendship with my daughter, my choices are to live backward into what I regret or live forward into what I want. If I think we have a problem communicating, I can dwell on that. But if I want a future in which she and I are friends, all I have to do is whisper softly to myself the word *friends* when I see her and my behavior is entirely different. Soon I am kidding around and having fun with her. Soon I am listening to her, as friends often do.

#39 Give It Away To Keep It

The Sea of Galilee has an outlet. It gets to give. It gathers in its riches that it may pour them out again to fertilize the Jordan plain. But the Dead Sea with the same water makes horror. For the Dead Sea has no outlet. It gets to keep.

—Harry Emerson Fosdick

Giving is a process that works with such startling efficiency that people are constantly amazed by the results they get when they use it.

I remember almost two decades ago when I joined a self-help group to recover from an addiction, one of their key ideas was "you've got to give it away to keep it." The point was that new-found freedom from addiction was a gift that you can only keep by giving away.

So we made a point of helping others recover. We gave our time and shared our own experience, strength, and hope so that others could find the courage to live without their own addiction. Soon they found they could do it and enjoy it. They were pleasantly surprised, to say the least. But to keep it they, too, had to give it away. They, too, had to share it with others, or it would disappear for them. Like a chain of love, they had to take great care not to break it.

This chain of love is a fundamental law of the universe. It doesn't just relate to addiction, it relates to everything. It relates to happiness. People who give it away keep it.

Make someone happy. Just one someone happy. And then you will be happy, too.

Most people think these ideas about giving have no practical value. That they are for saints and altruists. But that's what's so deceptive and exciting about giving. It has *huge* practical value.

In his marvelous book *Circle of Innovation*, business guru Tom Peters devotes an entire section to the power of giving. He recounts how the book that made him famous became a best-seller. When he finished the manuscript for *In Search of Excellence*, he sent free copies to every top business executive he could think of. His publisher thought he was crazy, giving free books to the very people they were targeting as his buying public. But Tom Peters believed intuitively in the concept of *giving it away to keep it*. His intuition paid off. The book became an instant word-of-mouth sensation among the people he sent it to, and the first business book ever to climb to the top of the *New York Times* best-seller list.

Book marketing consultant John Kremer recounts in his newsletters how the William Morrow publishing company used the giving principle to create another best-seller. When they sent out 5,000 galleys of their new novel *Morning's Gate* to booksellers, they also enclosed a letter asking those booksellers to return a postcard giving the name and address of a favorite customer. Six hundred booksellers responded to that offer. Morrow then sent those 600 readers autographed copies of the finished book. Not only did this program generate word of mouth among the readers, but it also pleased the booksellers who were able to do something nice for their customers.

It was yet another of the billions of examples of the practical power of giving. We get what we give, in business and in life.

#**40**   Think Skill

The successful warrior is the
average person with laser-like focus.

—Bruce Lee

The first step to connecting with another person is to think of listening as a skill.

This isn't as easy as it might seem. If you don't believe me, try this experiment: Go to your family or your friends, or your team at work, and ask someone whether they are as good a listener today as they were three years ago. Most people will be confused by your question. They won't know what you mean. They might even think you are trying to criticize their listening.

I've had people say to me when I've asked them that question, "Well, I think so. I mean, I had my hearing checked last year when I took the company physical and it was fine."

I've had other people say, "I don't know what you mean. Don't you think I'm listening to you?"

Now I'd like you to notice something. Would we have gotten the same kind of confusion if we had asked them whether they were a better tennis player or golfer than they were three years ago? Most people know exactly how much better or worse they are with golf or tennis than they were three years ago. Why? *Because those are things that we hold in our minds as skills.*

Most people don't hold listening as a skill. To most people, listening is completely passive—something they have to *endure* until it's their turn to talk.

But if we were willing—from this moment on—to hold listening as a skill, relationships would alter immediately. Just from that one change in thinking, relationships would be less out of control.

After finishing an important conversation, we could now ask ourselves, "On a scale of one to 10, how well did I listen?" That's a skill question.

We could even continue to review our performance: "Could I do better next time? Did I ask any good questions? Did I make sure they knew I was listening? Am I getting better? Am I noticing more?"

Most people just *react* when someone else is talking. They react emotionally and unconsciously. That's their habit. But it's only a habit. By being willing to notice how we are listening, we can start to create the new habit of listening skillfully. Skillful listening is not an unconscious emotional reaction. It's a conscious and thoughtful action.

#41 Eliminate Preoccupation

The immature mind hops from one thing to another.
The mature mind seeks to follow through.

—Harry A. Overstreet

Preoccupation is the enemy of all achievement.

It doesn't matter what the activity is, preoccupation is the enemy. The activity could be listening or cooking or free-throw shooting or poker playing or lovemaking—preoccupation is the enemy. Preoccupation diminishes all achievement.

Preoccupied listening is the same. It's a kind of listening that we all do from time to time, but once we catch ourselves doing it, it's helpful to stop it, because it is *always* damaging to the relationship. It's a kind of listening that dishonors and demeans the other person in the conversation.

Preoccupied listening means that I might *appear* to be listening to you, but I'm actually thinking of other things. Although I may be nodding and making my many listening faces and my subtle listening noises, I'm preoccupied with other ideas in my head. I'm listening more to my inner voices than I am to your voice.

We all know those listening faces we put on and those listening noises we make: "Mmm-hum...right...un-huh...exactly...there you go!"—but we're not really listening. We're preoccupied with other thoughts. Perhaps we're preparing our defense to what's been said earlier, or perhaps we're thinking of dinner plans. It's all preoccupation, and it's all damaging to the relationship because the other person can always sense the preoccupation.

If I listen to you in a preoccupied way, you will always go away feeling vaguely dishonored. If someone were to ask you later about your conversation with me, they might say, "Did you talk to Steve?"

"Yes," you would hesitate to say.

"Well, did he listen to you?"

"Yes, I guess he listened."

"Well, what's the matter?"

"Oh I don't know, I just don't seem to connect with him. I guess it just must be chemistry. I don't feel the connection when I talk to him. I don't even know why."

Well, *we* know why. It's called preoccupied listening and whenever we catch ourselves listening that way it's a good idea to stop it. With gentle repetitious practice, we can get good at bringing ourselves back into the conversation. We can bring ourselves back into focus. Each time we bring ourselves back, we get better at it. That's what a skill is. Like hitting a ball with a good follow-through. We can listen with a good follow-through. In relationships, that's how we connect.

#42 Eliminate Prejudice

Real difficulties can be overcome.
It is only the imaginary ones that are unconquerable.

—Theodore N. Vail

Another type of listening that is damaging to relationships is prejudicial listening.

The root word in prejudicial is "pre-judge." Every act of prejudice is an intellectual mistake because it's a premature act—a premature expression of ignorant opinions. Prejudice is, by definition, judging something before the evidence has been presented. Therefore, all prejudice is a mental mistake, and prejudicial listening is no different.

If I listen prejudicially to you, I am judging what you're going to say before you even say it! In my gut I already feel what you are going to say. You have something to say to me, but because I think I already know what it is, I'm not really listening. I already know what you are saying.

What if you came to see me and I said, "Come on in and have a seat. I already know what you are going to say."

You would hate that. You would know that you had no chance of communicating with me.

Prejudicial listening is a very common cause of relationship breakdown. It's also the cause of some strange experiences. See if this ever happens to you:

"I already told you about that," you say.

"No, you didn't," I say.

"Yes, I know I did. I've told you about that, in fact more than once."

"You're crazy. If I had known about this, I'd never have put Binky to sleep. I know you never told me about it."

"I told you. You were sitting right here when I told you."

"Never. I would have remembered. It's something I know I would have remembered."

"I'm willing to take a lie detector test."

This kind of confusing conversation happens all the time when prejudicial listening has become the norm. The reason I didn't hear you is because I felt I already knew what you were saying.

People who listen this way have already set up a filter in their minds. They already interpret what you are saying even before you've had a chance to say it.

Let's say that my prejudicial listening filter thinks you are critical of me as a parent. That's what I *already hear* in what you say before you even say it.

"You didn't pick up our son at school today," you say.
"Did I give you the wrong day on my message last week?"

"I what? Oh my....oh no, well I don't know. Are you saying you think I did that on purpose?"

"No, I'm just...."

"...so, you're saying I am so irresponsible as a....."

"No. I'm just trying to sort out....."

"You're saying I shouldn't have custody any more, you're saying I'm a bad parent, right?"

"...No....just that he wasn't picked up, and when they called me...."

"Oh! I get it. You're saying that they call you because they know not to call me anymore because I'm too irresponsible to even return their call. You're saying you want full custody now? That you want to meet me in court and take all my rights away?"

I might be exaggerating here, but I might not be. People often hear what they *think* they hear and not what is really being said. And that's prejudicial and a shame.

#43　Get Engaged

*It is better to be happy for the moment and be burned up with
beauty than to live a long time and be bored all the while.*

—Logan Pearsall Smith

When people are young and immature, their minds are always
going on "out of body" excursions. It's hard for them to stay
focused on any given conversation. You often see kids' eyes glaze
over when you talk to them for more than a few seconds.

But as young people mature, it is possible for them to gain
more and more control over their roving minds. Soon they can reel
themselves in and settle down to really listen to someone else. Soon
their minds are experiencing the poet Rilke's "stillness like the
heart of a rose." That's when relationships get better and better.

The best ways to create relationships are also the best ways to
listen to people. That's because listening creates such an immediate bond.

The kind of listening it's most fun to keep practicing is *engaged*
listening. In that format, when I'm listening, I'm totally engaged—
like gears in a machine are engaged—totally locked into what you
are saying.

A few years ago in one of our seminars, a guy at the back of the
room raised his hand and said, "Hey, Steve. I think I know what

you mean by engaged listening. When I was engaged to my wife, I listened to her a lot differently than I do now."

That was his idea of engaged listening. He wasn't far off, because humor rarely is. If you really think about it, he was probably more correct than I realized as I laughed at him and mocked his observation.

When we are in the process of falling in love, we're using the full scope of our imaginations to listen with. Somehow, during courtship, we drop the habitual worry and fire up the imagination again and use it like we did when we were children—to create with, and be clever, and be thoughtful and imaginative. So we listen differently, too. What would be a boring night of talk to other people, in courtship becomes some enchanted evening. We listen with all we've got. We listen in a way that honors and adores the other person. In more ways than one, we tend to become engaged.

I can only get better and better at engaged listening through repetition. When I find my mind has left the room, I simply bring it back. I repeat this process every time it happens. Pretty soon bringing it back gets easier and easier, like reeling in a fish. After practice, I can even catch the fish on its way out of the room. Soon I can even catch it right at the point of impulse, as it's *considering* leaving the room.

It's harder to think about practice than it is to actually practice. That's because we think of practice as boring and dread sets in. Practice is the last thing we want recommended to us. But practice, in itself, really isn't boring. What's truly boring is *thinking about practicing* ahead of time.

Once I'm actually practicing something, I know I am getting better at it. I can sense it and feel it. Repetition increases skill. And anything I'm getting better at becomes more and more fun to do. This is especially true of engaged listening.

#44 Listen Creatively

Everything in the universe is within you.
Ask all from yourself.

—Rumi, Persian Poet

The human mind is like a brightly-lit city at night.

There are great places to go, and there are not so great places to go. And people who allow their attention to wander off to dangerous parts of the city will eventually lie down at night in the gutter with broken bottles and a damp, whiskey-soaked cardboard box for a pillow.

But once we accept listening as an active skill and not just a passive experience, we can get very creative about where our minds go—and about how easily we can guide our attention.

The human mind doesn't have to just sit there when it listens. It knows how to actively reach out and grasp the meaning of the words that people are saying. It can listen in wildly creative and proactive ways, seizing the pictures painted by another's words.

Creative listening is sometimes like listening with a "save" button in front of you. Just as you can save something on your computer screen, you can also save something someone just said to you. You merely save it on the biocomputer screen. Then, when it's your turn to talk, you can refer directly to what's on the screen.

When it's your turn to talk, you can talk about what someone has just said to you.

Most people don't do that. They listen to what was said and then they fly off in a new direction. They pivot and fly. But creative listening asks that we stay focused. Soon we're using what has been said to build our own words on. We don't just *react* to what was said, we create something mutually enjoyable from it. We combine our words with the other person's. We weave them together in the most creative way.

My friend Fred Knipe and I used to play a poetry game that is a good illustration of creative listening. We would go to his cabin in the woods for a couple days to get away, and after a bottle of good convenience store white port to loosen us up, one of us would write a line of poetry on the typewriter on the wooden table. The other would then study the line, sometimes for a long, long time. Reading it, laughing out loud at it, standing up and pacing the room, lighting a long cigar, pouring more wine, and then finally typing the second line. Then it was the other "poet's" turn. We did this back and forth and back and forth for hours. Each line had to be based on and built on the line of the first person. It was great fun, and I must admit to actually turning some of the poetry in to a professor from whom I was taking a poetry writing class. (It never failed to receive anything but the strangest comments and most cautious grades.) The fun, though, was already experienced at the cabin. The fun was in the give and take, and more important, in the building on the other writer's words. It was quite an enjoyable experience.

To be a creative listener is a similar exercise and also quite an enjoyable experience. And to ensure the creativity in the listening, it helps when I ask myself this question before the conversation begins: How can I make a difference with the person I am listening to?

Just before I am about to meet with someone I can always remember to gently allow my attention to alight on the difference I can make in that person's life.

If I am placing my attention on the difference I can make then I am no longer allowing my attention to be diverted and distracted by outside events. If I shine my light on the difference I can make in your life, then I cannot be, at that moment, distracted by my feelings. The more small differences I see that I can make, the more my confidence rises. The more my confidence rises, the easier it is to listen to you.

#45 Just Be Straight

You can't wake a person who is pretending to be asleep.

—Navajo Proverb

A lot of times you hear people lying to themselves and you are struck by how those lies harm their relationships.

One of those lies is, "I'm not good with people."

I was brought in to consult with a company that sold office equipment and after a successful series of sessions with the sales staffs I was asked if I would bring the same relationship training in to the technicians on the service teams.

"I don't know if you could do it," the vice president of service said to me, "and of course you would have to change a lot of your seminar."

"Why?" I asked.

"Well, because these are service guys," he laughed. "We're techies. We're typically not that good with people."

"That's not true," I said.

"Yes it is true," he said. "You're used to working with salespeople. Salespeople are great with people. They're backslappers who know how to yuk it up and tell jokes and schmooze and all that. They're fraternity type guys. They're slick and smooth. We're just average Joes. We work for a living."

"All the better for relationships," I said.

"How do you mean?"

"Well, you tell me. Would you rather spend your time with a backslapping sales type, or with an average person?"

"Well, I'm prejudiced. I like technicians. But we can be the shy type. We can be introverted, focused on machines and not people."

"That will be part of your charm," I said. "That's part of your appeal to your customers. You are real. You're not phony. You're absolutely focused on getting the job done for them, and being simple and direct about it. If you're shy and clumsy, they'll love you all the more. Just keep your promises and exceed your service expectations, and people will love you. We'll have a great relationship seminar, and I won't change a thing in it. You'll get shown exactly the same ways to create great relationships that salespeople get. They will work for you as well if not better."

"But what about service reps not being good with people?"

"That is a lie."

"A lie?"

"Right. A lie."

All self-deception is an attempt to avoid some action—some action that you imagine will be uncomfortable. Some of the things the service techs would learn in the seminar about creating relationships might have caused some discomfort to execute at the beginning, but when they took it slowly, in small steps, and they were gentle and easy with themselves, they became great. They were basically pretending not to be good at relationships to avoid some actions they needed to take to become great.

We lie to stay out of action. Just like salespeople often lie about not being mechanically inclined. It's not that they're bad with technology, as they say, they just don't want to take the action of learning it. The function of the lie is to make a person passive and to justify the passivity.

The seminars with the service techs went extremely well and they all laughed and nodded knowingly when I began the day by asking them to confess that they were lying when they said they were not good with people.

"If your daughter asks you for a hug when you come home, do you refuse?" I asked them in the course. "Do you tell her you are not good with people?"

Deep down, everyone is good with people.

#46 Jump Into Action

Regret for the things we did can be tempered by time. It is regret for the things we did not do that is inconsolable.

—Sydney J. Harris

Colin Wilson once pointed out that a sure way to cure people of feeling depressed would be to throw them down a flight of stairs.

Their feelings would change immediately.

In this age of compassion, sensitivity, and reverence for depression, that would probably not be a popular sentiment. But inside the idea is something worth considering.

One day Steve Hardison invited me to his home for lunch and conversation and he spent some of our time together explaining his system of personal coaching. Given his huge influence on my life, it was fun to listen to him talk about his personal coaching theory.

"It's all about action," he said. "People's relationship problems can all be traced to a lack of willingness to take action. If I can get someone into action, I know my coaching will be successful."

"What if it's not the right action?" I asked.

"It's not a matter of right and wrong so much as it is a matter of being in action and not being in action," he said. "Let's say you come to me with a problem. If I can get you into action, *any kind of action*, the magnitude of the problem will start to diminish right away."

We were at his kitchen table enjoying sandwiches when he gestured toward his backyard, which we could see through the picture window.

"Let's say you come to me with a problem in your life and we go out back here to talk about it. And as you're describing your problem to me I have a little ball I am throwing across the lawn and asking you to go get for me. As you talk, I keep tossing the ball out there, and you're telling me this huge problem in your life as you go get the ball and bring it back to me each time. And as you go out and return each time, your problem is getting smaller and smaller in your mind. If I had asked you to rate your happiness in this matter on a scale of one to 10 before we started discussing it, you might have said it was a two or a three. I guarantee you that after retrieving the ball for me over and over you would rate your feelings about this problem much higher."

"Like getting a dog to fetch?" I said.

"Yes," he laughed.

"Well, what would that action have to do with this particular problem?"

"That's my point!" he said. "You asked if action would be valuable if it wasn't the right action, and I am saying action is what is missing, not doing the right thing. So, obviously, fetching a ball wouldn't relate to much, but your problem would diminish in your mind. It would become more manageable to you."

Think of someone right now. Have it be a person that you have a difficult relationship with in business or in personal life. Now, immediately, take some kind of action. Get on the phone with them to acknowledge something, send them an e-mail of gratitude for something, make an appointment to see them, anything. Any action will do. And then sit back and evaluate. How did you feel about this relationship when you first thought of the person? How do you feel about it now?

#47 Turn Inside Out

Inside you there is an artist you don't know about.
Say yes quickly, if you know, if you've known it
from before the beginning of the universe.

—Rumi

I could tell the woman was ticked off by the way she looked when she approached me. I was getting ready for a speech to a large group of people and was having some trouble clipping my microphone on as I stood by the side of the stage.

"Do you have a minute?" she said.

"Sure," I said, finally just throwing the little microphone to the floor and looking up at her.

"I read your latest book," she said, "and I don't agree with you."

"That's fine with me," I said.

"You said to listen to the universe. You said the universe would tell you...whisper to you or something about what your soul's purpose should be. You said the next time you feel joy, just notice and that's your soul trying to tell you what you should be doing with your life."

"Yes, I did say that."

"Well," she said, "I did that...I felt real joy when I loved someone, but after a long period of continued rejection, I no longer

169

agree with you. That only brings pain and sadness. So, having known my true purpose and never having it realized, I'm not happy, but quite sad and angry. I'm tired of all the disappointments in life. Just pretending to jack yourself up all the time with motivational books, speakers, et cetera only prolongs full realization of the truth—you can't always have what you really want. Perhaps that's what growing up really means."

"Maybe that's what Mick Jagger meant," I said, trying to lighten up the conversation a little.

"Mick Jagger? I love Mick Jagger. What do you mean?"

"You can't always get what you want, but if you try sometime, you just might find, you get what you need."

"So you don't disagree with me that your book is a bunch of nonsense?"

"I do disagree with you about some of the things you said."

"Like what?"

"Like thinking another person, someone you think you've fallen for, can be your soul's true purpose in life. That's not what my book meant. That it could be another person. I meant *your* purpose. Your true life's work. What you love no matter what people are saying to you at the time. Besides, why would you want the kind of person who would reject you, anyway?"

"I felt joy when I was with him. You said to listen to that."

"I didn't mean glandular joy. I meant the joy you feel when you yourself are *doing* something. It always comes when you're making some kind of difference. It's the joy of difference-making, it's not the joy of being approved of by some other person. That's not joy. That's a temporary satisfaction of a neurotic need."

"Oh, so I'm a neurotic?"

"Where he is concerned, it sounds like you are."

"Thanks for building me up."

"I can't . . .I don't have the power to build you up," I said. "I can't build you up. Only you can build you up. And that's exactly where you have misinterpreted the book."

"So there's something fundamentally wrong with me."

"No! That's just it. There's nothing wrong with you at all. What's happening is a simple mistake that's easy for you to correct unless you're so into this guy that you can't listen right now."

"I'm listening."

"In your head there is a computer. Let's call it a biocomputer. Let's call it your brain. You have this biocomputer and you are using it incorrectly, which is why you aren't getting the result you are looking for. Let's say the result you are looking for is a life of fulfillment and joy."

"That's good enough for now."

"Okay, if that's what you are looking for then you are going about it in the wrong way. You are searching on your computer for the wrong thing. You are searching for some other person to give you those feelings and as you've found out, that other person is not a reliable source for those feelings. In fact, he is a more reliable source for the feeling of rejection right now."

"I follow you so far."

"So you are using this wonderful search engine you've got, called the *imagination,* the wrong way. You are using it to worry with. When, in reality, it was installed in your computer for something else entirely. It is supposed to be used to create with. Worry is a misuse of the imagination."

"Worry is a misuse of the imagination?"

"Right."

"So what am I worried about?"

"You are worried about everything! You are worried about life's disappointments. You are worried about sadness and anger. You are worried about your love not getting returned. You are worried about being rejected. You are using your imagination to worry with."

"Haven't you ever been rejected?"

"I have felt that way. I have *felt* rejected many times, but I have never *been* rejected. And neither have you. Humans don't have that power over us. Why would we want to give someone that kind of power? All you have really is the feeling of rejection, and that's caused by no one else. That's caused by your imagination."

"How is that?" she said.

"If someone doesn't want to see me, I don't have to have that mean that I've been rejected. I can have that mean that they are stupid. Or that they don't get who I am. Or that they are on a different path. Some people are just clueless. Just realize that the guy you're talking about is simply clueless."

How to use the artist in you

"So what about my purpose and my joy?"

I told her to go inside, not outside. To take care of herself first.

"Create your own life," I said. "Make a difference in others' lives by *your* life's work and when you start doing that, your self-esteem will rise up so high you won't need someone's else's approval so desperately. You'll have your own. We look for love in all the wrong places. Love will come to you when you've got your life together. Not the other way around. Most people are like you and want it to be the other way around. They think their life will get together when they find someone to love. They've got it reversed."

"I think I might be seeing what you mean. Do you mind if we talk after your speech?"

I could tell by watching her walk away that she was feeling much better. Especially compared to what she looked like when she first approached me. And it wasn't that I'm such a magician with words that it turned her around. Anyone can turn anyone around. Anyone can cheer anyone else up. It really wouldn't have mattered what I said to her as long as I could get her to snap out of her worry for a minute and start creating some better pictures in her mind. I think she took a moment to picture what she wanted her life to be about and that altered her mood.

That's often how we can cheer someone up. Somehow we get them to see their own power to create. Sometimes it's by appreciating the creating they've already done. Sometimes it's by telling personal stories that empathize.

But whatever we do, they eventually see that they can't be creating and worried at the same time. They can't be creating and depressed at the same time. Because you use the same section (the imagination) of the biocomputer for both things. If it's busy doing one thing, it can't do the other. If it's busy creating, it can't worry.

That's really our basis for optimism. Not that outside events are wonderful, but that inside processes are wonderful. Not that we are going to get outside approval, but that we are going to get inside approval. Given our fundamental knowledge of how the imagination works, optimism is not a stretch. In fact, optimism is the easiest and most logical position to live from.

After my speech, the same woman came up to see me again. This time she was looking a little friendlier.

"Do you realize you contradicted yourself?" she said.

"Really?" I said. "Well, it wouldn't be the first time. How did I do it?"

"Well, you told me before the speech to find my happiness inside, right? And then in the speech you said that people got happy by looking outside themselves to see what kind of a difference they could make to others. To see what they could *give*. So which is it? Inside or outside? I think I was looking outside and trying to give to this guy, but he kept rejecting me."

"You weren't looking outside to give, you were looking outside to *get*." I said, wondering if I understood it myself.

"Okay, so I was. But what about the contradiction?"

"Really, there's no contradiction. First look within, then look without. Look inside to find your intention. Find your purpose. What are the differences you want to make? What kind of difference-making makes you feel happy? That's inside you. Then once you've got that, look outside, and get busy."

#48 Learn to Say No

Self-respect is the fruit of discipline;
the sense of dignity grows with the ability to say no to oneself.

—Abraham Heschel

Many people get sidetracked into designing and drawing up all kinds of wish lists in their lives without stopping to say *no* to what they really don't want.

In relationships, it's important to say no. "No! I will not accept that. I will not be with someone who cheats on me, who disrespects me, who abuses me in any way." That kind of "no" is a more powerful stand than all the wishes in the world.

Taking a stand against what I don't want is even more robust and decisive than trying to figure out what I do want.

Often when I am working with people trying to construct goals and missions we go way off track when we attempt to imagine what it is we want. However, when we start at what it is we *don't* want (in this company, in this relationship, in this home) then we get clear and decisive. Then what we do want emerges of its own logic and beauty.

I once worked with a company in New Zealand that got off track every time some money was accumulated. Every time things got prosperous, the company leaders' minds wandered, and soon they were looking for easy quick ways to get even richer. It was only when things got bad that the company returned back to being clear and decisive.

The strongest statement ever made by the company's president was when the company had struggled long enough in her eyes and she declared to everyone who would listen, "No! We will *not ever for any reason* have even one more unprofitable month. I will do whatever it takes to make certain we *never* lose money again."

After years and years of saying yes to all kinds of money-making ideas that usually didn't work, she finally gathered the strength to say *no* to something. It was the most powerful and effective thing she had ever done as a leader.

"No" is the strongest of all words. Because by saying no, you are taking a stand. You are staking all your life's energy on stopping something. You are drawing a line in the sand. It's the strongest language we have to use, because it's the most powerfully decisive thought a human can think.

I have watched and lived and worked with people who wasted their lives on a seemingly hopeless and incurable addiction to alcohol. Then they wake up one day after hitting a low enough bottom and simply say no. That one word becomes the strongest word they ever said because it changes their lives completely.

Later, the people would invent complicated sentiments about saying yes to a higher power or to sobriety or to freedom and love and peace and kindness. But all of that is just invented frosting when compared to the raw irrevocable power of the time they said no. No more. Not one more drink.

Tasting the fruit of discipline

The company president I referred to who said no to losing money went on a streak of profitable months that turned her entire company around. That's how powerful "no" is. But some-how, along the way, she got lost again. And instead of focusing on her one huge stand against unprofitable spending, she began to be seduced by "yes" again. Soon she was saying yes to all sorts of speculative schemes. She hired people who promised her the moon but never delivered. She was once again fueling her company on wishes and hopes, but nothing that resembled a strong stand. She was saying yes to everything. Breathlessly voicing yes's: "Oh Yes, yes, yes, yes, yes," until everyone was intoxicated and confused. The company lost all focus and began engaging in businesses that it had no skill in whatsoever. And, as always happens with anyone who can't say no, the world crashed in all around them. All her best people began leaving. The company shrunk down to a tenth of its former size. And outside observers of the company began predicting bankruptcy.

But right there in the midst of all this doom came a long-lost abandoned word. The most powerful word a human can utter. A word that was uttered by our cave man ancestor at the door of his cave to keep the saber-toothed tiger from harming his children: "No!"

The president took a stand. She said no to going under. She was down to almost no people left, the entire sales staff had left, and she still had the courage and depth of soul to cry out "No!" We will not collapse. We will not go down.

And so she became the whole sales staff herself. She went on calls all day and worked tirelessly to build things back up. Fu-eled by one small and powerful word, she kept the wolves at bay. Soon there was a very large check in the mail and her company had new life.

Is the lesson learned? I really don't know. If all of her brain-storming sessions and team meetings have drifted over to "yes" again, then it may be that she will never know. She may need a few more lifetimes to really see the difference between the two words. The power of the one, and the dreaminess of the other. But my prayer is that she finally gets it and will often ask herself and her team what it is that they will no longer tolerate. That would be the strongest thing she could do. Because only from that stand on the word "no" can the "yes's" of future growth and innovation be built.

Often when people are having difficulty negotiating something it is helpful to return them to the core strength of no. What is it that you absolutely do not want? What won't you tolerate? Once the no's are all on the table, the yes's often emerge and become obvious. But when we hide the no's they fester inside us as primordial urges and fears. Soon the secret knowledge of them undermines a long negotiation full of wishes and hopes and empty dreams.

In all relationship-building, it's most effective to first take a stand against what you don't want and will not accept. For example, if I would love to have a romantic relationship in my life, the best thing I can do is first take a stand against its opposite.

Because if I spend all my time wishing and hoping and dreaming of what I would like to have, I'll probably carry those wishes into the nursing home with me.

If, however, I wake up one day and realize that I am lonely and not making a difference anywhere and not enjoying any part of this solitary life in which all I do creatively is try to figure out how to entertain or pamper myself today then I might have worked up enough inner strength to say the strongest word there is in this situation, "No!" No to this life. No to this isolation. No to this loneliness. I'm ending it. It's over. I won't permit it in my life for another minute.

And then, emboldened by my stand, I will head out the door to meet people and help people and connect with people everywhere I can.

#49 Create Your Voice

As soon as you trust yourself,
you will know how to live.

—Johann von Goethe

The most important relationship to create is the one you have with yourself. Without starting there, you can't relate effectively to others.

You can have the relationship with yourself be anything you want it to be. It's not locked in to past hurts and memories. Not if you don't want it to be.

Start with asking yourself a question: How do I talk to myself? As a friend? Or do I use the tone of voice of a disappointed parent?

Most people keep hearing a worn-out parental or teacher's voice in their head and try to listen to that voice as if it were the voice of their conscience. It is *not* the voice of their conscience; it is the voice of past hurts and memories. It is not left in the head because it guides us well; it is left in the head for no good reason at all. It is left in there because when it was first heard, the mind had no shape yet. The child's mind was soft and tender and the voice was driven through the ear repeatedly with a mallet.

But when we see through that voice and learn to live beyond it, the best thing we can do is create a new voice. We can create an internal counselor who is on *our* side. We can create a voice that talks to us as a friend would. It becomes the voice of a solid supporter.

If we leave in the old worn-out voice of past hurts and humiliations as the voice of our conscience, then all we hear all day is, "That was stupid. Why haven't you done that yet? You're totally disorganized. You should have known that would happen. This is what you get for not being in shape. How could you feel good with the way you eat? No wonder they don't like you, you never spend any time with them. Oh, no, look at what you forgot, you're lucky your head is tied on or you'd forget that too. You never leave in time. You're too lazy to ever amount to much. What a mess you've gotten us into this time. You don't deserve that kind of happiness. Why is everyone else doing so well financially? What's wrong with you? You should be ashamed of yourself."

The ironic thing about an inner voice like that is that we listen to it all day without ever talking back.

If our mother-in-law ever talked to us that way, we would throw a fit. If our mother-in-law were to say anything as negative about us as we say all day in our heads, we would defend ourselves all night long. We'd fight back. And we would be right and we would believe it.

The most creative act we perform in adulthood is the creation of an optimistic voice inside. Who we are to ourselves determines who we are to others. It's impossible to be happy with other people if deep down we're not happy with ourselves. It all starts there.

This voice works better:

"You had a great day yesterday. You accomplished a lot in a short time. That was a good connection you made with your daughter. You really care about her and she knows it. You don't just say things; you're really there for her. You've got a few challenges to face today, but they're nothing you can't handle. Let's take them one at a time. Let's take it easy and see if we can't do something interesting and clever. Let's slow down and have some fun today. You always find a good way to solve these things. You've got a lot going for you. Even when you're physically tired, you can see things through. You're a finisher. You have a lot to be proud of. Let's get into action on some things. And let's have some laughs. Repeat: You can be sincere, but you don't have to be serious. You have a wonderful way of seeing the humor in everything. Let's play a game and see how much of this we can finish by early afternoon. Maybe even knock off early and see that movie you wanted to see. I'm here for you. I'm always by your side. I'm your best self. I'm the part you call on in a crisis, but I can work for you in a non-crisis, too. I'm always here. I'll always support you. Keep smiling. Keep laughing. Keep dancing. Keep singing. This is your life. You are the star of this movie and the script is good."

A voice like that will change your life. And the good thing about it is that it does not require anything external to happen for you to create it. You don't have to wait for the right time, or for the right teacher to come along. You can do it right here, right now. You can start this very minute. Put this book down and talk to yourself about all the things that are good about you. Have *that* be your voice from now on, and when you hear the other voice, as you will, just talk back to it. Talk it down. Support yourself against that voice. Take *your* side from this day on.

#50 Give from the Spirit

*Now we sit together
and I can't think of a thing to feel.*

—William Olsen

Vision of a Storm Cloud

Giving comes from the spirit, not from the heart.

Giving from the heart is sold to us as the only meaningful kind of giving, but I recommend that we not buy that story anymore. Giving from the heart implies that we should always wait until our emotions are correct, until we *feel like* giving. If we don't, the theory goes, it won't be real.

But that's not at all true. In fact, it's so false it's hilarious. It's a kind of cultural superstition that has hung around for years and it's a superstition that keeps people from building relationships.

The best gifts come from the mind and the imagination (which is to say the human spirit). When someone is really touched by a gift you never hear them say, "My what an emotional gift!" What they always say is how *thoughtful* it was.

The more thought I put into what I'm going to give another person, the better the relationship gets.

But if I wait until I *feel* like giving, someday I may sit straight up in my death bed shouting "Whoa! Time out! Can I do that

182

over? My life? Can I do my life over? Because something just occurred to me. My father. There were things I could have given my father, especially in his later years. A picture of my son playing basketball. I was always going to give it to him because he himself used to play basketball, and I thought about making a photo montage of a picture of my father and my son, where they cross-focus into each other. My father would have loved that. He would have had tears in his eyes. And he would have realized that everything he did in his life led to this beautiful boy of mine, named after him, and now playing the same sport he played. But I never had time. I always put it off. Or I would allow an old father-son resentment to come up and soon I didn't *feel like* giving anything to my father. What a waste of life that was. What a missed opportunity. All the time I spent worrying, I could have been giving. All the time I wasted *feeding* off my own emotional ups and downs, I could have spent that time thinking about contributing to others."

Don't wait for your heart to tell you when to give. Use your mind. Give it some thought. Jot down some notes. Go for a walk. Let your mind and spirit conspire to plan a way to make someone happy.

*"If only you could love enough,
you would be the most
powerful person in the world."*

—Emmet Fox

✂ Index

❧ About the Author

Steve Chandler is a keynote speaker and seminar leader who is famous worldwide in his public presentations for being, as PBS described him, "an insane combination of Jerry Seinfeld and Anthony Robbins."

Chandler is also the author of *100 Ways To Motivate Yourself, Reinventing Yourself* and *17 Lies That Are Holding You Back*. He lives with his wife and family in Arizona, and can be reached at 100Ways@Compuserve.com.